Ron Keller has a unique ability in developing strategic road maps that assist executives as well as entire corporations get from where they are presently to where they want to be, with the least amount of stress!

Reverend Steve Baran
President, National Christian Counselors Association (NCCA)

Ron Keller has made a remarkable impact on my life in the two decades we have worked together. Through temperament analysis, he has taught me to know who I am, to play to my strengths and appreciate the gifts I was born with to make a difference in this world. I am forever grateful for his wisdom and guidance; he has helped me unlock my door of "potential" to take a higher road in life.

Joe Grabowski
CEO, Wenck Enterprises, Inc.

Over 40 years ago, in the halls of my local high school, the genesis of this book emerged from the real-life conversations Ron Keller was having with students like me... a kid who was trying to make sense of it all and figure out a course and direction for my life. Turns out that the principles and steps Ron laid out 40 years ago still make sense today and at all stages of life. I am so thankful for his personal and written wisdom in my life.

Dale Preszler
Retired Business Leader, YoungLife Volunteer Area Committee Chair

Ron Keller is one of the people who have had the biggest positive impact on my personal and professional life. At every one of life's major hurdles, Ron's discernment and knowledge has provided truth and clarity, separating the artificial from the real issues. Ron has a gift of seeking to understand people and their issues, posing thoughtful questions, and creating a paradigm shift in thinking. He has done this for me on many occasions and this wisdom and guidance is now available through this book. He is a true blessing to all who come into his teachings.

Chris Maxson
CEO & Owner, Maxson Companies

Ron Keller's wisdom and expertise have been invaluable to both of us over the past 10 years. Without question, we owe much of our success in marriage, family, ministry, career and leadership to his unique insight and guidance.

Eric & Kelly Dykstra
Lead Pastors, The Crossing Church

Ron Keller's personal counseling, books and friendship have had a profoundly positive impact on my life, to such a degree that I can't imagine what my life would have been like without it. This book will help you leverage Ron's deep experience, wisdom and grace-filled understanding so that you can find the personal mission God has created for you.

Matthew O'Keefe
Ph.D., Teacher, Entrepreneur and Engineer

I've known Ron Keller for over twenty years and have had the privilege of working with him for some of those years. Ron has a unique gift of helping people in person or in writing. Regardless of where they are at on their journey, he can help them discover their course for life, setting them on a healthy trajectory. I have experienced this in my own life, and witnessed it in the lives of countless others.

Greg Seeger
Manager of Community Engagement, Thrivent

Ron Keller is a man after God's own heart! Ron is more than an inspiration; he is a gift to many people. He has changed many lives, including mine. His calm, laid back spirit is so welcoming, and that coupled with the gifts he has been blessed with has helped people in rich and mighty ways. This comes through his writing, making you feel as though you're sitting down with a wise friend. He and this book are a true blessing in this world!

Melissa Halleland
Real Estate Consultant, Edina Realty Rochester

DISCOVER YOUR COURSE FOR LIFE

ONE STEP AT A TIME

RON KELLER, PH.D.

WESTBOW
PRESS®
A DIVISION OF THOMAS NELSON
& ZONDERVAN

Some Scripture quotations are from the New King James Version of the Bible. Copyright © 1979, 1980, 1982, Thomas Nelson, Inc., Publishers. Other references to the Scriptures are paraphrases of passages from J.B. Phillips, Today's English Version, Jerusalem Bible, and New International Bible Hyper-Bible.

To assure ultimate confidentiality, none of the individuals referred to in this book are identified by their real names. Though the case studies are real, the situations are disguised and modified. These stories have been written and/or shared with the author orally so they may be used to encourage others in their life journeys. The situations described have been gathered from small group gatherings all over the United States.

Originally published as Twelve Steps to a New Day: an interactive recovery workbook for spiritual growth / by Ron Keller.

Author Photo: Lauren B. Photography

WestBow Press books may be ordered through booksellers or by contacting:

WestBow Press
A Division of Thomas Nelson & Zondervan
1663 Liberty Drive
Bloomington, IN 47403
www.westbowpress.com
1 (866) 928-1240

ISBN: 978-1-5127-3670-0 (sc)
ISBN: 978-1-5127-3671-7 (hc)
ISBN: 978-1-5127-3669-4 (e)

Library of Congress Control Number: 2016905597

Print information available on the last page.

WestBow Press rev. date: 7/6/2016

Contents

Dedication vii

Acknowledgments...ix

Why This Book? xi

Brief History and Invitation xv

Steps to discovering your course for life

1. I Admit that I am Powerless.. 1

2. I Can't Change Myself--But God Can 15

3. Surrender Leads to Serenity..................................... 26

4. Know Yourself to Love Yourself 44

5. Free At Last..61

6. Ready 69

7. Asking For Healing... 79

8. Sharing the Healing 88

9. Making Amends...101

10. Daily Review..111

11. My Most Important Daily Appointment 121

12. I Will Reach Out to Others...................................... 129

Steps to discovering your course for life with

        Scriptural references 143

Profile for Ron Keller, Ph.D. 147

More information about Ron Keller and Associates 149

Dedication

To my mother, Viola Margaret,
in recognition of her life-long
love, prayer, support, and
continuous encouragement

Acknowledgments

I am grateful for my family,
our children,
my mentors,
associates,
teachers,
and all of those who have invested in me.

I am grateful for many people who have helped me
in the writing and editing of this book,
especially the following:

Nancy Keller, my wife, for her loving patience
and prayerful encouragement.

Gail Steel, president of Prince of Peace Publishing, Inc.,
Burnsville, Minnesota, for her clear vision and
unwavering commitment to the success of
the first version of this project.

Janet Thoma for her consistent, positive, skillful,
and careful editing of the second version of this book.

For Britney Ahlmann and her timely, professional input into this book and the Discover Your Course for Life process.

DeWayne Herbrandson for enabling this project to take place by serving as agent and consultant.

The staff at Westbow Press for their patient and persistent encouragement in publishing the third version of this book.

Why This Book?

I have been in counseling, consulting, and leadership development for more than forty years. In all of those years, I have heard the persistent cry from people of all ages, in all walks of life: "There must be more to life." "I am stuck." "I feel trapped." "I don't have a life." "I need a new life."

My life, for the past forty-five years, has been dedicated to living that new life and helping others find it.

This book is a manual. It's a workbook. It's a course. It's a step-by-step guide to take you into a new life, a life that will exceed all of your greatest expectations.

It will help you discover a new lifestyle filled with hope and freedom.

This book is part of a thorough process entitled *Discover Your Course for Life.*

More information is available at our website: Ronkellerassociates.com.

You have probably been studying all of your life ... English, math, history, music. You might have a degree or two.

But have you ever taken a course in the study of yourself? A course that focuses on who you are? You already know it is more important to know yourself more than any other subject. If you don't know yourself, you most likely can't know what you should do to make the most of the gifts you have been given.

Imagine for a moment the joy and freedom you could experience when, without a doubt, you could look in the mirror and honestly, without hesitation say, *I know you ... I like you ... I love you. I will take good care of you because you have a very important purpose in this life.*

We as humans have been described as "fearfully and wonderfully" made. The Scriptures tell us that deep down our "soul" knows this very well. Using this book and the Discover process will help you get in touch and stay in touch with the real you—made and designed by God.

The steps used in this book will help you to get into the new life you have been designed to live. The steps are time tested. They offer the guaranteed promise of a new life. You take the steps, one at a time, and new life will come to you with each step.

The steps you will take in this book are based on simple principles rooted in hundreds of years of history and experience. They are based on biblical teaching combined with healthy common sense.

The first version of this book was published in 1989. A revised version was published by Thomas Nelson, Nashville, in 1993. Since 1997, the book has been self-published and has been translated into Spanish, Russian, Korean and Albanian, all by individuals needing the books to work with people in these countries.

There are no copyrights or royalties involved.

The book has been used by individuals and groups in schools, churches, home groups, corporate offices, and prisons.

Through the years, emails and letters have come from people everywhere to describe how the steps in this book have changed their lives.

As you take your first step, it is my prayer that you will discover the rich, new life you are invited to.

Brief History and Invitation

I started taking these steps when I was fifteen years old.

I am still taking a step every day ... still discovering new life with each step.

When I was a senior in high school, I took the first step after much struggle and hardship. Through my father's alcoholism, I learned that I am powerless. I could do nothing to change him, help him, or change my circumstances. What I could do is help myself, and the first step to doing that was admitting to myself, to God, and to another person that I am powerless.

Much relief came in taking that first step. There was and is much more relief to come with each reminder that I am powerless and with each step I take.

The book you have in your hands (or electronic device) is a compilation of my and many other people's stories and experiences, all pointing to the hope of discovering a new life.

The steps used in this book are adapted from the old twelve steps of Alcoholics Anonymous (AA). You will quickly discover you do not need to be an alcoholic to apply these steps to your own life.

The principles of the twelve steps have been with us for centuries. In the 1940's, the founders of Alcoholics Anonymous found a way to capsulize and distill those principles into a powerful process that has saved thousands (millions) of lives.

Those principles were never meant to be isolated and applied to only those who had addiction to alcohol. However, as time went on, the twelve steps and AA became synonymous. In other words, if you were using the twelve steps, you must be an alcoholic.

The stigma of being an alcoholic prevented most people from thinking there was any reason or need for them to learn about or apply the twelve-step lifestyle to themselves.

It's only in the past few years that authors like me have attempted to open the door for all of us—anyone—to embrace and reap the benefits of the twelve-step process. Some of these benefits include discovering the "abundant life," a better understanding of our purpose for life, day-by-day direction and guidance in investing our lives in those matters that are truly significant.

The principles of this book have eternal value. They will be forever relevant.

Helping each new generation understand and apply these principles has been a creative challenge and one of the reasons for this book in its third revision.

While the principles of this book have eternal value, they need continuous adaptation to stay one step ahead of the constant erosion that's taking place in our culture.

I have been in a full-time leadership role for more than forty-five years.

My role has included leadership training, teaching, management, coaching, marriage counseling, corporate consulting, ministry training, team building, pre-marriage counseling, spiritual direction, workshop/retreat leadership, curriculum design, writing, and speaking.

In all of these roles, my purpose has been the same. My role has been that of an ambassador, one who represents another, serving that person and that person's agenda. In all of these roles, the basic twelve-step and scriptural principles presented in this book have permeated my relationships and activities.

My desire and focus has always been on serving the One who first loved and served me.

In these forty-five years, I have felt an urgent and growing need to encourage and train creative and servant leaders who will have it as their goal to have their hearts, minds, and eyes clearly focused on our common leader, our Lord Jesus Christ, and His purpose for our lives.

The Promises of a New Life

If anyone is in a relationship with Jesus Christ, that person is a new creation, the old has passed away and *the new has come.*

—2 Corinthians 5:17

I have come to bring you life, life in all its fullness.

—John 10:10

Chapter 1

I ADMIT

THAT I AM

POWERLESS

Step 1:

I admit that I am

---

powerless over certain

---

parts of my life and I

---

need God's help.

When I was a teenager, the biggest problem I had to live with every day was my dad's drinking. He was an alcoholic. I never knew what to expect from him. Would he be drunk or sober? Did he mean what he was saying, or didn't he? Could I count on him or not? Would he embarrass me?

His alcoholism affected me in many ways. I was scared of him and his disease. I was afraid about what was happening to him, our family, and me. I felt I always had to be on guard. I missed having a father. When I was fifteen, my dad went into treatment. I remember how lonely I was. I was afraid he wouldn't come back home.

It took me a long time to figure out I had no control over whether he'd come back or not. I realized there was nothing I could do about the situation. I couldn't change my dad. I could only change myself and the way I looked at things.

Step One helped me a great deal. It helped me to admit I was powerless over these circumstances. I had no power to change my dad, myself, or my situation.

I thought about that feeling of powerlessness the night I visited a unique group when the leader said, "Could we please look at Step One together, and could someone read from the Bible, Matthew 6:25-34?"

We read together, "I admit that I am powerless over my life and that I need God's help." Then we proceeded to the reading in Matthew.

After the readings, the leaders divided us into small groups of four and then guided our discussion with questions. More and deeper sharing took place there as we all talked in depth about our issues and how we were dealing with them in light of Step One.

"This step helps me to admit my need for God's help," one of the group's participants said. "I am very powerless over my financial situation right now. I have not been irresponsible in spending; I simply don't have enough money to pay my rent. I have to let go of trying to make it all work. I have done my best, and now I need to trust God."

After about forty-five minutes of sharing in small groups, the leader invited us back to the larger group. "I would like to take a few minutes to reflect with you on Step One," she said. "This step asks me to honestly admit to who I am and the way I do things. It asks me to own my life, my lifestyle, and my problems. It asks me to face my life as it really is. This step urges me to surrender to God those things, circumstances, and people that I am powerless over."

Everyone listened intently as she went on. "This step invites me to slow down, gently shed my masks, and get into my heart. It invites me to come to God, who loves me and who longs to embrace me just as I am.

"This is not a self-help step or a self-help group. This group is for people who have had a taste of powerlessness and know that only God can help them. I have been working on this step almost every day this past week. Mostly, I have had to acknowledge my powerlessness over my health."

The leader was a thirty-five-year-old mother who had three children at home. She had cystic fibrosis.

"Sometimes I get bitter about my health. I think about how unfair it is that I have this disease. But one day at a time, I accept this problem and the impact it has on me and my family."

She went on to say, "Jesus loves to help. I know from my own experience. He asks, 'What do you want Me to do for you?' (Luke 18:40). The first step in getting help is admitting that I am powerless and that I need God's help. This past week, I told Him I needed encouragement. He has given it to me."

Several in the group spent a few minutes in brief, faith-filled prayers for this leader's expressed need. There was prayer for others in the room. The meeting was concluded. Most people hung around a while longer.

As I walked to my car, I felt encouraged. I realized I had been in privileged company. People from a variety of backgrounds and educations came together on that night to share their lives with each other. What a great model it was. These people admitted they were powerless over certain parts of their lives, which is a dilemma we all share.

Everyone Is Powerless over Something

At a recent dinner, a friend asked several of us, "What do any of you feel you can control?

"When I was younger," he went on, "I used to think I had power over everything. Now that I'm forty, I feel powerless over most things. I can ultimately do little about my health. I can't do anything to control my wife or kids. At work, I'm really at the mercy of the economy—I could lose my job any day. And I feel powerless about what is happening to our environment."

At the other end of the table a friend said she resented the use of the word *powerless.*

"That word made me feel like I was supposed to give up, lie down like a rug, and let everybody walk all over me. It made me feel like a loser. I have been abused and powerless many times in my life. I didn't want any more powerlessness. The word made me angry.

"And then I experienced its real meaning. I had reached the end of my rope with my son. He was eighteen and wanted to do life his way. I had been fighting to keep control of him. Gradually, I came to understand that I am powerless over him. He has his own life to live now. I have done my best for him. The powerlessness is not weakness but strength. I feel strong because I have chosen to surrender him to God."

She went on to say she'd learned appropriate detachment. "Detachment is letting go, surrendering, and turning things over to God. Detachment is learning to take care of myself and to be less concerned with the way my son is or what he does. Detachment, for me, is admitting powerlessness and accepting things as they are. Jesus Christ is the ultimate model of self-surrender and powerlessness for me."

We are all powerless over some thing, person, or situation that comes uninvited to our minds and seeks to dominate, control, or be in the center of our lives at the present moment. On the following pages, you will be given a number of suggestions of people, situations, or things that might seek to "control" you. The key to overcoming these "addictions" is to identify the areas you are powerless over (90 percent of the solution to any problem is proper diagnosis) and then admit them to yourself and someone else.

It's one thing to know our problems and issues. It's quite another to admit that we have them and that we are powerless to change them.

Sometimes we blame others for the way we are. Our parents are common targets. But at some point in our lives, we need to take full responsibility for who we are. They did their part. We must now do ours.

When I was younger, I often used my father's alcoholism as an excuse. I had a reason to feel sorry for myself. I could blame him for some of the hard circumstances in my life. Fortunately, for the last five years of his life, my dad and I had a good relationship. I discovered many of his good qualities that I had not previously recognized. Our relationship had an unusually good ending, partly because I took responsibility for my own life and feelings. Eventually I came to realize that all of us face some hard circumstances. Until I went to Alateen (a group for teenage children of alcoholics), I thought my situation was unusual. Now I know that all people have struggles.

I am still learning to live with the fact that I will always be powerless over certain parts of my life. Being powerless means I am without power, force, or energy. It means I am weak about some things and that I am not able to produce any effect or change. I am powerless over some of my own personality defects. I am powerless over my God-given temperament. I'm a perfectionist. I'm an ideal-aholic (I think everything should be ideal). I am a workaholic.

I still admit, daily, my need for God's help. Life would be hopeless without God's intervention and ultimate control in my life. I need His help, today more than ever, in little and big things.

How about you?

To help you get started in identifying what you might be powerless over, please check which of the following areas seem to be problems, addictions, or challenges for you right now. You may check one or several, or add your own.

___ My cell phone	___ Taking care of myself
___ Codependence	___ Being in a crisis
___ Feeling guilty	___ Being too independent
___ Work	___ Being too dependent
___ Relationships	___ Sex
___ Chocolate	___ Being too "routinized"
___ Facebook	___ Being too "spiritual"
___ Food	___ Being preoccupied
___ Gambling	___ Fear
___ Smoking	___ Drugs
___ Sports	___ TV/videos/movies/video games
___ Denial	___ Excitement
___ My dreams	___ Fantasies
___ Complacency	___ Caffeine
___ Clothes	___ Myself
___ Being overwhelmed	___ My "helping" others
___ Lists like this	___ An affair (inappropriate emotional or
___ Being judgmental	physical bonding)
___ Websites	___ Stability/security

___	My "stuff"	___	Money
___	Shopping	___	The unknown
___	Moving up	___	Houses/property
___	Anxiety	___	Fatigue
___	Fixing myself	___	Perfectionism
___	Controlling/manipulating	___	Anger
___	Stress	___	Depression
___	A lifestyle		

___ _____   ___ _____

___ _____   ___ _____

Now, from the list below, please check which of the following creates the most anxiety in your life.

1. My biggest problem right now is

___ My self-confidence

___ My spouse

___ My child/children

___ My job

___ My peers

___ My relationship with God

___ Finances

___ My future

___ Secrets I am carrying around

___ My unresolved past

___ _____

    As you think about your problems and the lists above, please read the following. This reading is taken from the book of Matthew and is one of Jesus's most important teachings on how to live a healthy life. It is part of what is referred to as the Sermon on the Mount. It is also His classic address on "letting go," the dominant theme of the first of the Twelve Steps.

I, Jesus, am telling you not to worry about your life and what you are to eat, nor about your body and what kind of clothes you are to wear. Surely life means more than food, and the body more than clothing! Look at the birds in the sky. They don't sow or reap or gather into barns; yet the Lord feeds them. Are you not worth much more than they are?

Can any of you, for all your worrying, add one single minute to your life span? And why worry about clothing? Think of the flowers growing in the fields; they never have to work or spin, yet I assure you that not even Solomon in all his royal garb was robed like one of these. Now if that is how God clothes the grass that is there today and thrown into the furnace tomorrow, will the Lord not much more look after you, you of little faith?

So do not worry; do not say, "What are we to eat? What are we to drink? How are we to be clothed?" It is the non believers who set their hearts on all these things. Your heavenly Master knows you need them all. Set your hearts first on the Lord's kingdom and righteousness, and all these other things will be given you as well.

So, don't worry about tomorrow: tomorrow will take care of itself. Each day has enough trouble of its own (based on Matthew 6:25–34).

Now answer the following questions, which are based on this reading.

1. Describe a situation in which you felt powerless. What did it feel like?

_____

_____

What did you do about it?

_____

_____

Did you ask for God's help? What happened?

_____

_____

What is Jesus inviting you to do in light of the reading from Matthew?

_____

_____

What the Bible says about Step One: A few reminders

I admit I am powerless over certain parts of my life and that I need God's help.

Choose one passage from the selections given below, and read it each day during the next week. Think about the passage by checking the statements that reflect your feelings.

1. In this well-known verse, David assures us that when the Lord is our shepherd, we have all that we need. Step One urges us to admit our need for God. Psalm 23:1

    The LORD is my shepherd; I shall not want.

___ I can't say whether this is true for me or not

___ The Lord is my shepherd. He has provided. He will provide. I trust Him.

___ It's really hard for me to trust anyone.

2. Written by Solomon, a man thought to be the wisest king who ever lived, these verses instruct us to depend on God and not our own abilities. Proverbs 3:5–7

Trust in the LORD with all your heart,
And do not lean not on your own understanding;
In all your ways acknowledge Him,
And He will direct your paths.
Do not be wise in your own eyes;
Fear the LORD and stay away from evil.

____ It is hard for me to give up control. I want to be in control.

____ Instead of trying to analyze situations or trying to make them go my way, I will trust the Lord with all my heart and let the outcome be in His hands.

____ It is hard for me to believe I can't figure things out on my own and that I need to trust God for His judgment and intervention.

____ It is hard for me to admit my powerlessness.

3. In one of Jesus's final hours on earth, he apparently was given a glimpse of the hell he was about to go through. His agony drove him to pray the prayer below. Matthew 26:39

Jesus went a little farther and fell on His face, and prayed, saying "O My Father, if it is possible, let this cup pass from Me; nevertheless, not as I will, but as You will."

____ It was different for Jesus. He didn't really experience powerlessness.

____ I am thankful I have a Savior who understands powerlessness.

____ I have experienced powerlessness in my life. I know what this feels like.

____ Jesus encountered a trial that He chose to give over to His Father. In my powerlessness I, too, choose to give my life over to God.

4. Paul reminds his Roman friends that we are all powerless, sinners, and in need of rescue. Jesus came at just the right time, Paul says. Romans 5:6, 8

    When we were still without strength, in due time Christ died for all ... But God demonstrates His own love toward us, in that while we were still sinners, Christ died for us.

____ Jesus came into the world at just the right time and for people who are powerless.

____ I am a sinner. I need Jesus.

____ Jesus Christ comes to help me in my powerlessness. He comes to me while I am in my human struggle to control my own life and future.

5. Paul is reminding the Christians in Philippi that they can survive anything, including the lack of food and money. Step One lets us rest in truth that "we are weak, but He is strong." Philippians 4:13

    I can do all things through Christ who strengthens me.

____ I cannot rely on anyone else's strength.

____ This passage has been true for me: I can do all things through Christ who strengthens me.

____ When I try to deal with my "stuff" on my own, I quickly get exhausted. When I ask for God's help, Christ strengthens me to endure all things.

Living Step One: The Challenge

Your purpose for life will be challenging. Part of the challenge is a willingness to admit you are powerless.

I was sitting in on one of our typical small group training sessions when the participants were sharing their experiences with Step One.

"The most difficult part of doing Step One for me is admitting to what makes me feel powerless. I don't know why for sure, but it's very hard for me to admit to anything," one person in the group said.

"I was raised to solve my own problems. I was taught to depend on no one except myself. I am a self-reliant person. It's hard for me to trust God or anyone with my problems," another participant said.

"So what does all this admitting stuff mean to you?" a group participant asked me directly.

From my perspective, admitting to who we are and admitting to our need is essential to having a healthy life. Admitting, to me, means several things:

1. *It means I am willing to be who I am.* I stop playing games. I get out of denial and stop pretending I can do life on my own. I accept my humanness, my struggles and pain.
2. *Admitting means I can be where I am.* I don't have to work so hard to be somewhere else. Most of my life has been spent in being where I thought I should be, rather than being where I am. This is a subtle form of denial.
3. *Admitting is surrendering.* I can let go, turning the struggle over to God and letting the outcome be His.

    It can be reflected in a prayer like this: *God, this is what life is like for me right now. Here is what I am feeling. This is who I really am. Thank you for giving me the courage to be who I am.*

4. *Admitting is a form of trusting.* The only way I can really make progress in life is to learn to trust myself, others, God, and my circumstances. That means saying to myself, *The way life is for me now is the way life is supposed to be for me now.*

5. *Admitting is accepting things as they are, not as I would like them to be.* Before I can do anything to change things, I need to accept them as they are.

    When I do not accept reality, I am living in denial. I am looking for a fix before I have dealt with why the problems are there in the first place. This step allows me to relax and let God do what needs to be done without me and my intervention.

6. *Admitting means I confess my sins, failure, and need.* I sometimes resent my powerlessness. I would like to be in better control of some of the events in my life. This is competing with God. Only God can be God. He is ultimately in control.

7. *Admitting is discovering that Jesus Christ is with me and that He will never leave me, as He has promised.* He is present, whether I like it or not. The sooner I admit to His presence and acknowledge it, the healthier I become.

As I made each of these seven points in the group, the participants shared their own experiences and feelings. Many of them had experienced this admission and shared the benefits they enjoyed from living this way.

"I find relief, peace, and serenity when I admit to who I am and to what is happening in my life. I get really stressed out when I try to deny things," one young woman said.

"I feel pressure build up inside me when I try to exercise my own power and fix things. When I admit to my powerlessness, I feel relief," said another.

13

Making Step One My Own

This section provides you with a format for integrating your feelings, responses to questions, and what you learned from this step, the Scriptures, and in your group meetings.

Date, day, and time of your writings: _____

1. At this point in my life, the major area that I am working on (For instance, I have discovered that I want to be in control of my life. It is hard for me to admit powerlessness or weakness. I have become aware of how much influence my father's workaholism has had on me.):

_____

_____

2. Major insights I was given into my life through this step (By listening to others, I learned that it is okay to be who I am; I don't need to play games or pretend.):

_____

_____

_____

_____

3. The strongest feeling I have had as I have worked this step (Relief—it's okay for me to be human.):

_____

4. The action I feel called to take as a result of working this step (I am now going to work at being more relaxed and less in control.):

_____

Chapter 2

I Can't

Change

Myself--

But God Can

Step 2:

I am coming to believe that

Jesus Christ came in a human

---

body, that He is here with me

---

now in Spirit, and that He has

---

the power to change my

---

weaknesses into strengths.

When a neighbor lost his job, he felt hopeless about his future. He was worried about how his family would survive without his income.

He had grown up in a family with a very strong work ethic. In his relationships, the important people were the ones who had accumulated wealth. "They were the ones," he said, "who had power and influence.

"What I learned is that my value comes from what I do," he explained. "In my family, no one ever asks or thinks about who you are; they want to know what you do, and then they make up their minds about whether you're an important person or not."

Our purpose for life is much bigger than what we can see, measure, calculate, or imagine.

"They think I am valuable when I have power over others. If you don't have money or power, you aren't a very important person in our family."

Many in my neighbor's group were nodding their heads. They knew what he was talking about.

This was a new discovery for my jobless neighbor. He had felt this stuff but had never before said it out loud. In the last four months, he had been learning how to say these things in this group. As he said them, he felt better about himself.

"So here I am without a job. I feel worthless. I'm embarrassed to let my parents know that I've lost my job. I don't like that."

Over a period of weeks, my neighbor unpacked parts of his life and got to the heart of some of his repressed feelings. It became clear that his self-image was based on performance. If he could do things well and accomplish many things, he felt acceptable to himself and others.

My neighbor, like many adults, had been convinced by the cultural standards of our time that we are lovable and valuable when we keep up with fashion trends, have a specific type of education, know certain people, own specific things, live in a specific neighborhood, and have a high income.

These cultural standards have been handed down from one generation to the next. For healthy relationships to take place in the family, someone will need to break and then change this pattern. The Scriptures teach us that "by grace you have been saved through faith, and that not of yourselves [your work]; it is the gift of God, not of works, to prevent anyone from being proud or boasting" (Ephesians 2:8–9). The world teaches us to earn our salvation (and everything else). The Scriptures teach us that all of these are gifts.

Changes do not come easily. When we've been programmed in a specific way from early childhood on, it will not be easy to deprogram.

The easy fix for my neighbor would have been to rush out and keep trying to get another job. To get healthy, my neighbor needed more than that. He needed to deal with the hard issues that prevented him from having a healthy self-image whether he had a good job or not.

Others in his group shared what God was doing in their lives to transform their weaknesses.

"I used to feel lonely all the time. I hate being lonely. But God has come to me, and He is changing my loneliness," one group participant said.

"I've had major health problems," another said. "I've taken each physical weakness to the Lord and He has healed or He is healing me."

"For months I had been exhausted. I know part of that came from my busy schedule, but a part of it was unexplainable. I needed energy and vitality. I asked God for His help, and He gave it to me," another participant said.

In each of these people's lives, Jesus Christ is doing miracles. They give the credit to Him because they have tried to change themselves and they have failed time and time again. Then He has come to help. He has the power to change them.

How do you feel about this second step?

Step Two--I am coming to believe that Jesus Christ came in a human body, that He is here with me now in Spirit, and that He has the power to change my weaknesses into strengths--is an important step for those who have doubts about God. Sometimes problems are so great that it hardly seems possible God cares. Step Two lets us say with integrity, "Where is God in all this?"

Step Two affirms three simple truths:

1. Jesus Christ did miracles when He was here in human form.
2. Jesus Christ is the same yesterday, today, and forever.
3. Jesus will do miracles in our time.

1. Jesus Christ did miracles when He was here in human form

If you need healing, there's no better place to look than in the first four books of the New Testament--Matthew, Mark, Luke, and John. It's often said that these books tell the story of the Great Healer. And that Great Healer is Jesus Christ.

Consider this story, which is just one of many.

There was a wedding at Cana in Galilee. Mary, the mother of Jesus, was there, and Jesus and His disciples had also been invited. When the hosts ran out of wine at the wedding, Jesus's mother said to the servants, "Do whatever he tells you."

There were six stone water jars standing there. Each could hold twenty or thirty gallons. Jesus said to the servants, "Fill the jars with water," and they filled them to the brim. "Draw some out now," He told them, "and take it to the steward."

They did this. The steward, who knew nothing about what had happened, tasted the water, and it had turned into wine. He called the bridegroom and said, "People generally serve the best wine first and keep the cheaper sort till the guests have had plenty to drink; but you have kept the best wine till now."

This was the first of the signs given by Jesus. He let His glory be seen, and His disciples believed in Him (based on John 2:1–11).

After reading about Jesus Christ changing the water into wine I

___ feel discouraged. This incident was for His lifetime only.

___ am hopeful. If He can change water into wine, He can change my weaknesses into strengths.

___ wish He would do a major miracle in my life.

___ wish I could have been at the wedding party.

2. Jesus Christ is the same yesterday, today, and forever

This is the promise Jesus gave to all of His followers in Hebrews 13:8. He will never change. He has the same ability and power today as He did when He expressed Himself in human form.

He created the universe. All that has been created was created by, for, and through Him. He expressed Himself by taking on human form. He came for sinners, the lost, and those who are sick.

He does the same today. He comes for the needy. He forgives sin. He finds the lost, and He heals those who are sick.

And He promised He will be this way forever. He will never change. Everything else around us may change. Jesus Christ will never change.

Before any of us can take Step Two, we must know who Jesus is. He told us about Himself in the Bible.

1. Jesus said, "I am the bread of life" (John 6:35).
2. Jesus said, "I am the light of the world" (John 9:5).
3. Jesus said, "I am the resurrection and the life. He who believes in Me, though he may die, he shall live" (John 11:25).
4. Jesus said, "I am the way, the truth, and the life. No one comes to the Father except through Me" (John 14:6).
5. Jesus said, "I am the true vine" (John 15:1).

For centuries these promises have given hope and encouragement to those who have felt powerless and hopeless.

3. Jesus will do miracles in our time

After His life on earth, Jesus continued to do miracles through His followers in the early church, as recorded in various passages in the book of Acts. All through history, believers have affirmed His miraculous intervention in their lives.

Today many people speak convincingly of miracles they have experienced. Those three people in my neighbor's group were just a few of the thousands of people in groups throughout the country who tell the same story: "I asked God for His help, and He gave it to me."

We can't do anything about certain parts of our lives, but Jesus Christ can. If He can change water into wine, He can change the difficulties we have.

Jesus Christ has the power to change our weaknesses into strengths.

What the Bible says about Step Two

I am coming to believe that Jesus Christ came in a human body, that He is here with me now in Spirit, and that He has the power to change my weaknesses into strengths.

As you read the passages below, check the response that seems most applicable to you at this time:

1. The crowds had jumped into several boats and followed Jesus after he had multiplied the fishes and loaves. He told them not to work for food that cannot last. "They said to Him, 'What shall we do, that we may work the works of God?' Jesus answered ... 'This is the word of God, that you believe in Him whom He sent'" (John 6:28–29).

___ For me, believing in Jesus comes easily.

___ Believing in Jesus is a real struggle for me.

___ I believe with my mind, but I do not trust Jesus with my heart and daily life.

___ I want to trust in Jesus Christ with all my heart.

___ Trusting that His will is being done is very difficult for me when I am in "survival" mode.

2. Jesus tells His disciples that the good news, His presence as Savior of the world, is revealed to the simple. "And He turned to His disciples and said privately, 'Blessed are the eyes which see the things you see; for I tell you that many prophets and kings have desired to see what you see, and have not seen it, and to hear what you hear, and have not heard it'" (Luke 10:23, 24).

___ I can see Jesus clearly. I know who He is, and I see Him at work in my life.

___ I want to see Jesus more clearly. I am open to hearing His voice.

___ I am afraid to open my eyes to Jesus.

___ I am so grateful God has given me the eyes to see who Jesus is.

___ Even though I do not see Him clearly, I do have faith in His presence and His ability to help me today.

3. In his first letter, John reminds his readers that Jesus Christ came to deliver us from sin, self-destruction, and death. He not only has the power to change my weaknesses into strengths, He has the power to give me eternal life. "And this is the testimony: that God has given us eternal life, and this life is in His Son. He who has the Son has life; he who does not have the Son of God does not have life. These

things I have written to you who believe in the name of the Son of God, that you may know that you have eternal life" (1 John 5:11–13).

___ I still believe eternal life is something I earn.

___ I still believe eternal life is a reward I get for avoiding certain things.

___ I believe I have been given eternal life in Jesus Christ.

___ I am afraid of this whole idea.

___ I know I have eternal life because of what Jesus has done for me. This gift He has given me regardless of my weaknesses.

Step Two lets us be where we are. It does not push us to say something that isn't true for us. It lets us slow down, evaluate where we are, and be honest with ourselves. It is a reminder that this is a process, not an overnight fix. We are gradually coming into a deeper faith in Jesus Christ. We are gradually getting a better understanding of what His coming and presence can mean to us.

Where are you in this process? Check the statements below that reflect your feelings:

1. The beginning of Step Two says, "I am coming to believe."

    ___ I fight this. I do not want to believe. I want to see; I am a doubter.

    ___ I am a doubter, but I want this part of my life to change.

    ___ This is true for me. I recognize I am in the process of becoming a stronger believer.

    ___ I feel secure in my faith. My life experience has taught me that I can believe.

2. That God, Creator of the universe, came to His own creation as a human person is:

    ___ beyond my comprehension.

____ I've never really thought about this much.

____ What difference does it make that God came as a human person?

____ This is the truth and I want to learn how to respond in worship and gratitude.

3. Jesus Christ is with me now in Spirit.

____ This makes no difference in the way I live my life, really.

____ I've never really thought about it.

____ I've always believed this.

____ I believe this, but this truth doesn't make much difference in the way I live my life.

____ I want to learn and do more about this.

Step Two assures us that it is okay to move toward belief, moving forward, knowing we will never completely arrive. We are "coming to believe." This means we are on the way. No one expects us to have perfect faith or be perfect persons. Our faith is perfected as our relationship with God grows, and our ability to trust God is strengthened through experiences with God

The following article affirms the power and impact Jesus's life has had on people in all of history.

One Solitary Life

Here is a man who was born in an obscure village ... the child of a peasant woman. He grew up in another obscure village ... He worked in a carpenter shop until He was thirty ... and then for three years He was an itinerant preacher.

He never wrote a book ... He never held an office ... He never owned a home ... He never had a family ... He never went to college ... He never put his foot inside a big city ... He never traveled more than two hundred miles from the place where He was born ... He never did one of the things that usually accompany greatness ... He had no credentials but Himself ... He had nothing to do with this world except the naked power of His divine manhood.

While He was still a young man, the tide of popular opinion turned against Him ... His friends ran away. One of them denied Him ... He was turned over to His enemies ... He went through the mockery of a trial ... He was nailed to a cross between two thieves ... His executioners gambled for the only piece of property He had on earth while He was dying ... and that was His coat.

When He was dead, He was taken down and laid in a borrowed grave through the pity of a friend.

Twenty centuries have come and gone, and today He is the centerpiece of the human race and the leader of the column of progress.

I am far within the mark when I say that all the armies that ever marched ... and all the navies that were built ... and all the parliaments that ever sat, and all the kings that ever reigned put together have not affected the life of people upon this earth as powerfully as has that One Solitary Life.

(Author unknown)

This second step, as described in "One Solitary Life," is the core of the Christian faith. God came to human beings as a human being. This is a crucial, pivotal, radical expression of love. This is grace, pure and rich. This is the greatest event in history.

Making Step Two My Own

This section provides you with a format for integrating your feelings, responses to questions, and what you learned from this step, the Scriptures, and in your group meetings.

Date, day, and time of your writings: _____

1. At this point in my life, the major area that I am working on (For instance, I know I need help in accepting the fact that God is present and involved in every aspect of my life:

_____

_____

2. Major insights I was given into my life through this step (I forget that God is present with me in this life. I don't even think about this.):

_____

_____

_____

_____

3. The strongest feeling I have had as I have worked this step (Excitement about having some things in my life finally get changed):

_____

4. The action I feel called to take as a result of working this step (Let God do the changing in me—stop trying to do it on my own; it doesn't work anyway.):

_____

Chapter 3

SURRENDER

LEADS TO

SERENITY

Step Three:

I turn my will and my

life over to Jesus Christ,

my Savior and Lord.

For several weeks I had been experiencing numbness and tingling on the left side of my body. I have generally been in good health. I had been jogging three miles several times a week.

Suddenly, these pains and sensations came out of nowhere, and my doctor, after doing all the tests he could, sent me to a neurologist. The neurologist ordered an overwhelming series of tests. I didn't know the body could be checked in so many ways.

First in the series were numerous blood tests, all of which turned out to be negative. These were followed by an EMG (shock and needles), a brain wave test, and two MRIs--a brain scan and a neck scan.

Hard as the test was, I had a great experience with the EMG. The attending technician was very compassionate, understanding, and helpful. After a brief explanation of the process she was about to put me through, she said, "You can do this test. The Lord will be with you." Her encouragement prompted me to ask if she was a Christian. "I've been a believer for many years. But only in the past few years has my faith been very strong."

"What happened?" I asked.

"I was doing a test like the one I'm doing on you," she said as she stuck another needle in my thigh. "The guy lying on this table had AIDS. He told us. Our whole office knew it. I was praying for him the whole time I was administering this test. And then I did a crazy thing. I accidentally poked myself with a needle that I had just taken out of his arm. I have never done anything like this before in my whole career."

She hesitated for a few moments as tears rolled down her face. "For six months, my life was hanging in the balance. I was immediately put on a medication to counteract the HIV virus, a medication that really messed up my body. And for that six months, we had to wait to know for sure whether I had been infected with AIDS. My husband and I spent many nights on our knees. I totally surrendered my life to Jesus Christ. I gave Him everything I had. I learned to live one day at a time, and I'm still doing it."

As she finished the tests on me, she told me the good news that up to this point her tests are still negative.

For several days before the MRI tests, my wife, Nancy, and I had been told about the two worst possibilities: (1) a malignant brain tumor or (2) multiple sclerosis. "Anything other than these two would be good news," Nancy said.

We both spent three nights "dreaming" about what might happen should either of these be the diagnosis. All we could do, with each thought, was surrender, turn my body over to Jesus Christ, and ask Him to do what must be done. I felt much liberation as I was able to let go of the outcome of the tests and my future--even if that future meant major surgery or confinement to a wheelchair.

I had heard about the infamous MRI "tunnel" and how difficult it is for claustrophobic people. Fortunately, I was not one of those people. My body was small enough to fit comfortably into the tight space.

When I lay helpless inside the tunnel for the MRI brain scan, I realized how helpless I was. I could do nothing but lie there and "let go"--let the technicians do what they needed to do; let the doctor do what he needed to do. All I could do was surrender and lie still. I survived the experience by imagining I was in the sleeping quarters of a great sailboat. I can tolerate anything related to sailing.

"The good news is you have a brain and it's fine," the neurologist reported three days after the test. "You have no tumor and no multiple sclerosis. The bad news is we still don't know what is causing these problems in your body, and so the testing will continue." (Translation: The torture will continue.)

The doctor has since discovered three degenerating disks in my neck, and these have caused the pain, the numbness, and the tingling. I had to stop jogging and learn ways to live with this until I went through with the essential surgery.

I have come to realize how terribly vulnerable and fragile I am. Many other challenging trials have taken me back to the same place: If I am to enjoy my life, I must give it to Jesus Christ.

At a group meeting, working on Step Three, several people described why they were afraid of taking this step.

"I am afraid," a young lady said, "that nothing will happen if I give my life to Jesus Christ. I would be devastated if God doesn't do something to respond to me when I give Him my life."

"I don't want to get religious," another woman said. "I've been around too many Jesus freaks, and they turn me off. I don't want to become like that, so that's why I hold back."

"Same with me," a young businessman said. "I don't want to be a zealous missionary in a foreign land and I have this feeling that if I give my life to God, He'll send me there. I don't want to go, so I hold back."

"God may or may not make great demands on our lives. It is His right to do so. We are His possession," one of the group leaders said.

"The core problem in life for all of us," she went on, "is that we ultimately want to be our own gods. We want to manage our own lives. Even if we do it poorly--running our lives right into the ground--we still prefer to be in control."

The message from our culture is simple and consistent: Be in control. "If you stay in control," our culture says, "you will have happiness, success, and prosperity."

"There are two fundamental realities in life," my friend's poster says. "Number one--there is a God. Number two--you are not Him." Step Three is a simple reminder of those fundamental realities.

You probably identified with some of the items on the list of addictions when you made Step One. Addictions are often our gods. We use them to fill the natural void inside us that should be filled by God. Addictions control us, like gods.

How can we displace these gods?

Jesus gave us two very clear answers:

1. You must become like little children. The kingdom of heaven is for those who become children.

When my son, Jonathan, was three years old, he became one of my main mentors. I used to think I would learn most from older people. That was at one time true. Now, I need to let younger people like Jonathan help me rediscover what life is really all about.

It was my spiritual director who first taught me about the need to become like a little child. "Let your son teach you how to do that," she said. "You will learn how to surrender and trust God by observing his trust in you." She was right. When I learned how to get down to Jonathan's level and let him give some leadership to our relationship, he showed me a whole other perspective on life that gave me more freedom from my anxiety.

2. Jesus said, "You must be born again" (be born from above). This is the second way to displace foreign gods. There's a story in the gospel of John that describes this more thoroughly.

A wealthy Pharisee named Nicodemus was one of the first people to be born again. He was a Pharisee, a leader in the Jewish religion. He came to talk privately with Jesus one night and said, "Rabbi, we know that You are a teacher who comes from God. No one could perform the signs that You do unless God was with Him."

Jesus answered, "I tell you the truth, unless a man is born from above, he cannot see the kingdom of God."

Nicodemus said, "How can a grown man be born? Can he go back into his mother's womb and be born a second time?"

Jesus replied, "Unless a man is born through water and the Spirit, he cannot enter the kingdom of God" (based on John 3:1-5).

How would you respond to this true story?

1. I think Nicodemus was
   ___ fed up with his lifestyle and sought Jesus for a better way of life.

____ a man who had heard just enough about Jesus that he wanted to meet Him face to face to check out whether Jesus might be the one he should give his life to.

____ a person who was drawn by the Holy Spirit to enter into a relationship with Jesus Christ.

____ I can identify with Nicodemus. He was a man a lot like me.

2. When I read "turn your will over to Jesus Christ," I am reminded of experiences in my own life when I

____ have fought this idea.

____ resented this notion that God wants my will and life.

____ have resisted the idea of turning my will over to Jesus Christ.

____ knew exactly what it meant to turn my will over to Jesus Christ but still did not do it.

____ did turn my will and life over to Jesus and I continue to do it.

3. Different denominations and schools of theology have their own expressions and cultural terms that try to grasp the meaning of Jesus's expression, "unless a person is born from above, he cannot see the kingdom of God." My experience with this expression has been that

____ I have been born from above (born again).

____ I want to be born from above (born again) but don't know what it's all about.

____ I guess this rebirth happened for me somewhere along the line.

____ I think this rebirth happened for me in my "confirmation" experience.

____ I feel like I am on the verge of some kind of spiritual rebirth right now.

____ I am open to rebirth but afraid.

4. Check the expressions below that best describe your understanding of being "born again."

____ This is a process. It is something that is still happening to me now.

____ Being born again marks the beginning of a new life, a fresh start, a turning point when I receive God's love.

____ This is the beginning of a new relationship with God. I see what God has done and is doing in my life.

____ This is the key to understanding the Scriptures.

____ This experience happens to each person in a different way.

____ This is something that all adults must decide about and experience on their own.

According to this passage, rebirth is not an option. Jesus says "unless a person is born from above, he cannot see the kingdom of God." This rebirth happens at God's initiative. God begins this process and accomplishes it by grace. We are the recipients of His acts of grace and kindness. The process begins and ends with God. It's part of what I have defined as the surrender cycle.

The Surrender Cycle

The surrender cycle is a process of becoming a whole person. This cycle has five phases:

Awareness

Admission

Struggle

Surrender

Serenity

In all of these phases, our choices are responses to Jesus's question to the paralyzed man at the pool of Bethsaida: "Do you want to be whole?"

To become whole, we need to be aware of our condition. We need to become more aware of our "addictions," compulsions, temperament, and personality traits. Because many people live in denial, they are not totally aware of their true condition. They avoid reality and stay in denial by watching TV or medicating their pain with chemicals, sex, or hyperactivity.

"For twenty-five years I was a driven man," a group member said. "At the expense of my relationship with my wife and children, I was determined to be successful in my work. Until I became aware that I am a bona fide perfectionist, nothing in my life could change."

His awareness came through pain. The older he got, the more anxious he felt about his life and career. He got physically sick from his psychological problems. He was headed for a breakdown until his wife finally intervened. She gave him an ultimatum: Change your lifestyle or you'll lose your family. At this point he took the necessary steps to change his life pattern.

Awareness comes in a variety of ways. Some become aware through prayer, loving companions who speak the truth to them, circumstances, and the Scriptures. In one of his letters, John wrote:

> If we say we have no sin in us, we are deceiving ourselves and refusing to admit the truth ... to say that we do not sin is to call God a liar. But if we acknowledge our sins, God, who is faithful and just, will forgive us our sins and cleanse us from all wrong.
>
> —based on 1 John 1:8–10

"All have sinned and fall short of the glory of God," Paul tells us in Romans 3:23.

All of us need to become more aware of who we are, of our temperament, and of how our behavior affects our relationships with God and others. This is difficult for most of us because we are creatures of habit. We are so well established in our patterns and lifestyles that we assume they are all okay--until something major happens to wake us up.

If we want to become whole, we must be alert to ourselves, others, and the circumstances in our lives.

Awareness is the first phase of becoming whole. Admitting our problem to ourselves, God, and another person is the second.

A young attorney began to work on his perfectionism with a professional counselor and in a group using this book. He discovered a long line of perfectionists in his family. He had always thought his family was ideal, but he was now discovering that many unspoken and unhealthy rules had been imposed on him.

He began to admit to himself and others the facts about his life. His family was not as ideal as he thought. It was not a bad family on the surface. But beneath the socially acceptable signals, there was much unaddressed turmoil and frustration.

For years, he had pretended that his father and grandfather had no flaws, foibles, or problems, that they were "perfect." They were his heroes and models. Now he was moving out of denial and admitting that they were human and had problems just like everyone else. This admission gave him the freedom and permission he needed to explore how their issues, subdued as they might have been, had affected him, especially in his perfectionism.

It was his verbal admission of this compulsion that helped him assess his life realistically. He then let go and let God go to work on changing this deficiency in his life.

"My whole identity is based on how well I can perform. I feel good about myself only when I am doing something really good-- and better than others can do it," he said. As he talked openly, the perfectionism lost its intense power over him. He realized he was not alone as others shared about performance-based identity. He felt hopeful about the changes that could take place in his life. Others in his group had walked the path before him and represented hopeful light at the end of the tunnel.

The psalmist apparently had a similar experience with denial and then admission. Perhaps many of the great saints and biblical heroes were more human than we recognize. As I have examined their lives more closely through the years, I have found them to be very human, and now I can relate to them better.

The psalmist said,

> *When I kept silent, (living in denial?) my bones were wasting away with groans, day in and day out; day and night Your hand lay heavy on me. At last, I admitted to You I had sinned, no longer concealing my guilt, I said, I will go to the Lord and confess my fault. And You, Lord, You have forgiven the wrong I did and have pardoned my sin.*
>
> —based on Psalm 32

After this young man admitted his perfectionism, he went through the next phase of the surrender cycle, the struggle to believe that his "diagnosis" was right. He began to rationalize: "Okay, so maybe I am a perfectionist, but it's really not so bad after all. I mean, who is hurt by my perfectionism? I could have worse problems, like alcoholism or drug addiction."

His family was on the edge of breaking up. He was taking medication for high blood pressure. He was frantic about his future. He had very few good friendships. All of these were clear indications that something was wrong with his lifestyle. Admitting to this was really hard for this young man. He wavered in his admission until he was thoroughly convinced that his compulsion would ultimately destroy him.

The struggle phase is perhaps the most difficult. Denial is a tremendous force that wants to keep us blinded and in bondage. The struggle to be honest and stay honest takes, to begin with, concentrated effort. With practice, this phase gets easier.

At this point, this young man moved into the surrender phase. Surrender is letting go, accepting who you are, coming to God and saying, "Lord, this is who I really am. This is the real me. I've had it. I'm fed up with the way I am. I need Your help, Lord Jesus."

Surrender means turning over to Jesus all that we discover about ourselves. It does not mean we give up and give in to our compulsions, problems, struggles, and issues. It means we turn them over, one by one, as they are brought forward in our lives, and we graciously let Jesus do what needs to be done, in His way and in His own good time.

We are told by the author of Hebrews to keep our eyes fixed on Jesus. Paul tells us in Colossians 3:1–3 to let our thoughts be on heavenly things, to look to Christ who is sitting at God's right hand.

The result and the final phase of this cycle is serenity. This fifth phase is a by-product that comes as we become aware of, admit, struggle through, and surrender our issues to the Lord.

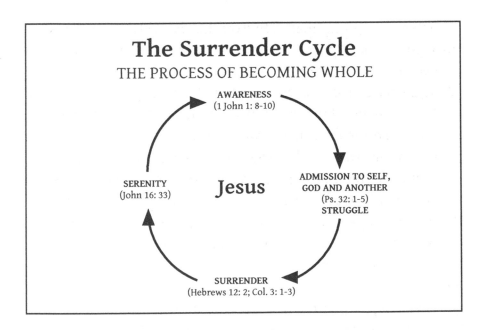

Many make the mistake of seeking serenity at all costs. This becomes the goal in their lives. They are often prey to trendy teaching and other "quick-fix" short cut ideas. Lasting peace and serenity come by going through all phases of the process and focusing clearly on Jesus Christ all along the way.

The more I have practiced using this cycle, the more serenity I have been given. This approach to life is now second nature to me––in major issues as well as minor difficulties.

Step One asks us to admit we are powerless over certain parts of our lives. It asks us to admit our need for God's help. We simply cannot change some situations, no matter how much effort we put into them.

Step Two acknowledges that although we may be powerless, Jesus Christ is not. This step reminds us that He is with us and can change our weaknesses into strengths. It asks that we "come to believe" in His power to change what we cannot change.

Step Three urges us to entrust our wills and lives to Him. It asks us to surrender to our Creator all that we have and all that we are. It is an action step, asking us to turn ourselves over to Jesus.

For some people, this is a very difficult step. Some may feel that they need to be successful in life, that they need to be self-sufficient. Others may feel it is a sign of weakness to ask for help. Still others believe surrender implies giving up. And many think that every part of their lives must be in order before they can even approach God.

In Step Three, surrender means giving my will and my life over to Jesus Christ, each day, each moment, just the way that I am. It is synonymous with seeking His presence, guidance, and counsel throughout the day. Surrender leads to serenity. The Serenity Prayer, brief as it is, best captures the surrender cycle.

> God,
> Grant me the serenity to accept the things I cannot change,
> courage to change the things I can
> and wisdom to know the difference,
> living one day at a time,

enjoying one moment at a time,
accepting hardship as a pathway to peace,
taking as Jesus did, this sinful world as it is,
not as I would have it,
trusting that You will make all things right
as I surrender to Your will,
so that I may be reasonably happy in this life
and supremely happy with You forever in the next.[1]

Please indicate the appropriate responses below:

1. Initially, this is my reaction to the Third Step:
____ It confuses me. I'm still not sure what this all means.
____ It makes me a little scared. I don't know what will happen next.
____ It makes me eager for more.
____ I want to wait and see and hear more before I say or do anything.
____ I have turned my will and life over to Jesus Christ to the best of my knowledge and ability.

2. Indicate where you are with this step:
____ I didn't know that Jesus wants my life.
____ I have given Him my will.
____ I have given Him my life.
____ I don't understand how to do this.
____ I'm interested but scared.
____ I don't know where I am with this step.

Who is in control of your life right now? To what or whom have you given permission to be the god of your life at this present moment?

---

[1] The first three lines of this prayer are most commonly used in A.A. circles. The prayer in its entirety has been attributed to Reinhold Niebuhr.

Years ago I remember hearing the expression, "Either you have surrendered to Jesus Christ or you're at war with Him." Today, I believe that I have surrendered to Jesus Christ *and* I am still occasionally at war with Him.

I admit that the god of my life can sometimes be my "ideal-aholism." At other times, my god can be my perfectionism. And there are the ever-present gods of materialism, longing for security, complacency, entitlement, and life's pleasures.

These are all battlegrounds for me. Will I surrender? Will I attempt to create my own destiny, or will I trust in His plan for my life? His plan is best, always.

What the Bible says about Step Three

I turn my will and my life over to Jesus Christ, my Lord and Savior.

Choose one passage from the selections given below and read it each day during the next week. Think about the passage by checking the statements below that reflect how you feel.

Now that we've looked more closely at who Jesus is, let's look at the invitation He gave to each of us.

1. After teaching His disciples about their mission, He spoke to all the people who would listen, and extended this invitation (Matthew 11:28-30):

    Come to Me, all you who labor and are heavy laden, and I will give you rest. Take My yoke upon you and learn from Me, for I am gentle and lowly in heart, and you will find rest for your souls. For My yoke is easy and My burden is light.

____ This is me. I'm tired. I'm ready to give my life over to Jesus Christ.

39

____ I want to know more about what Jesus's yoke would be like for me.

2. As he describes Jesus coming to us as a human being, John realistically lets us know that some people would not accept Jesus: "But as many as received Him, to them He gave the right to become children of God" (John 1:12).

____ At times in my life I have rejected Jesus Christ.
____ Since I have received Jesus Christ into my life, I have been given the power to be one of His children.
____ I would like to learn more about what it means to be a child of God.

3. Paul describes what happens to the person who says yes to Jesus. Paul says, "Therefore, if anyone is in a relationship with Jesus Christ, he is a new creation; old things have passed away; behold, all things have become new" (2 Corinthians 5:17–21).

____ I know this is true for me. I am in a relationship with Jesus Christ. I am a new creation.
____ I am struggling with my old life.
____ I am in a relationship with Jesus Christ *and* I am struggling with my old self.

4. Our faith in Jesus Christ is what saves us, Paul says. No one can be justified by keeping the Law. My justification has taken place already because "I have been crucified with Christ; it is no longer I who live, but Christ lives in me; and the life which I now live in the flesh I live by faith in the Son of God, who loved me and gave Himself for me" (Galatians 2:20).

____ This passage is true for me. This is my experience.

___ I don't have to "play god." Jesus is my God. My old self has been crucified with Him. I can now live a life of faith pleasing to Him.

Taking Step Three is a choice we make freely and deliberately. It is a choice we make in stages. The more we get to know Jesus, the more we trust Him and give Him more of ourselves. Although this step may feel a bit scary, there's really nothing to be afraid of. Jesus Christ is the kindest, most gentle, and most loving person history has ever known. He can be trusted.

Step Three is important because much is at stake. You may decide not to turn your will and life over to Jesus. That means you have decided you will continue to be your own savior.

God loves you. He does have a plan for you. His plan is rich and full of life. When we turn ourselves over to our Creator, our lives are fulfilling. If we hold back, we may be missing out on the great things God has in store for us.

Ask Him to make Himself and His plan known to you. Your life will become more directed, and you will become more like Him. When you turn your will and life over to Jesus, you will know peace, His will, and your course for life.

A Surrender Prayer

Dear Lord Jesus Christ,
     You truly are my Lord and I am Your servant.
     I am sorry I so often get those two roles turned around. I want with all my heart to turn my will and my life over to You. I know I am unworthy of Your love, but I also know You know me and You came for people like me.
     I am one of those "independent spirits" who wants to do life my way. Please help me to let this go

41

so I can do life Your way. I want to be in a relationship with You.

Jesus, I'm afraid to give You my life. I've fought so long and hard to keep it. Just when I feel like I have it, I feel this tug inside to turn it back over to You. I know it would be best for me. Sometimes I feel so close. Please help me to surrender all of myself.

I want, Lord, to love You more than anything else. You have given me so much, Lord. Please grant me this one more request so that I may better serve You and others.

Making Step Three My Own

This section provides you with a format for integrating your feelings, responses to questions, and what you learned from this step, the Scriptures, and in your group meetings.

Date, day, and time of your writings: _____

1. At this point in my life, the major area that I am working on (For instance, identifying the ways in which I play god each day.):

_____

_____

2. Major insights I was given into my life through this step (I have been given the privilege of choice. I can turn my life over to God or I can try to run it by myself.):

_____

_____

_____

_____

3. The strongest feeling I have had as I have worked this step (Relief— it is good to surrender to God.):

_____

4. The action I feel called to take as a result of working this step (I plan to let go and let God do what needs to be done.):

_____

Chapter 4

KNOW YOURSELF

TO LOVE

YOURSELF

Step Four:

I begin honestly listing

---

what I know and discover

---

about myself: my strengths,

---

weaknesses, needs, and behavior.

This fourth step has been referred to as doing an inventory. This is much like an assessment that keeps track of what we have, what we've done, where we've been, and where we are now.

It is essential that we know our strengths, weaknesses, and needs. It is critical that we understand, appreciate, and respect who we are.

In my private counseling practice relationships, most people have somewhat of an understanding of who they are; very few have a sincere appreciation for who they are, and fewer have respect for themselves. Respecting ourselves means we know what we need, we have appropriate boundaries, and we do what we need to do to take good care of ourselves.

When we do not take care of ourselves and get our non-negotiable needs met, our hearts, minds, bodies, and souls suffer. God designed us with needs. An example of one need he has instilled in us is a need for dependence upon Him.

When our needs are not met, our behavior changes. In most cases that behavior borders on the unacceptable. Most of us have experienced bouts of bad behavior. Bad behavior is a symptom of unmet needs. It is not the problem.

Step Four invites us to do an inventory of our behavior and the consequences of our choices. It is also a helpful step to reset our trajectory for the future.

The fourth step gives us many clues about what our course for life should be. Often our deepest desires have been tucked away in our memories. It is possible to ignore the many times those memories re-surface to remind us that from early on, our desire was to be a nurse, teacher, musician, attorney, pastor, etc. Many of these dreams seemed unattainable way back when. We dismissed the idea and forfeited the opportunities we could have had.

Step Four helps us get back in touch with some of those dreams. Perhaps it's time to re-consider and move forward with the original course of action.

The following pages will help you do Step Four. No one expects you to complete these pages quickly. Take your time. Glance over these pages frequently and add to the lists you've begun. Set a realistic goal for yourself for a tentative completion date. Some people have spent years working on this step. The Bible gives us a good beginning point.

What the Bible says about Step Four

Jesus had an important conversation with a woman who discovered herself in the process. He reminded her of some things she had forgotten. She had chosen to forget some things that His simple presence brought to her mind.

He had left Judea and gone back to Galilee. This meant He had to cross Samaria, a country whose residents were not favorably inclined toward Jews. On the way, He came to the Samaritan town called Sychar, near the land that Jacob had given to his son Joseph. Jacob's well is there, and Jesus, tired from the journey, sat down by the well. It was about noon. His disciples had gone into the town to buy lunch. When a Samaritan woman came to draw water, Jesus said to her, "Give Me a drink."

The Samaritan woman said to Him, "What? You are a Jew and You ask me, a Samaritan woman, for a drink? Jews don't associate with Samaritans."

Jesus replied, "If you only knew what God is offering and Who it is that is saying to you: Give Me a drink, you would have been the one to ask and He would have given you living water."

"You have no bucket, sir," she answered, "and the well is deep: How could You get this living water? Are You a greater man than our father Jacob who gave us this well?"

"Whoever drinks this water will get thirsty again; but anyone who drinks the water that I give will never be thirsty again; the water that I give will turn into a spring inside him, welling up to eternal life."

"Sir," said the woman "give me some of that water so that I will never get thirsty and never have to come here again to get water."

"Go and call your husband," Jesus said to her, "and come back here."

The woman answered, "I have no husband."

He said to her, "You are right to say, 'I have no husband,' for although you have had five, the one you have now is not your husband. You spoke the truth there."

"I see you are some kind of prophet, sir," said the woman. "I know that Messiah, the Christ, is coming; and when He comes He will tell us everything."

"I who am speaking to you," said Jesus, "I am He."

The woman put down her water jar and hurried back to the town to tell the people, "Come and see a man who has told me everything I ever did; I wonder if he is the Christ." This brought people out of the town, and they started walking towards Him.

Many Samaritans of that town had believed in Him on the strength of the woman's testimony when she said, "He told me all I have ever done" (based on John 4:1–26).

Please answer the questions below; then proceed through the following pages writing down the first things that come to your mind in each category.

1. What impresses me most about this true story is:
    ____ that Jesus goes to a foreign territory (Samaria) to reach out.
    ____ that Jesus is not bound by the cultural mores of the day.
    ____ that Jesus expresses a need (for water).
    ____ the promise that Jesus gives to the woman.
    ____ the fact that Jesus reveals who He is.
    ____ Jesus's approach to the woman.

2. As far as I'm concerned, this story is about
    ____ the relationship of the Jews with the Samaritans.

____ water.

____ women.

____ Jesus knowing everything about us.

____ cultural norms.

____ all of the above.

3. If I had been the woman at the well and Jesus had told me He knew all about my personal life, I would have:

____ run scared.

____ bowed down in fear.

____ been embarrassed.

____ been relieved--finally someone knows the real me.

____ been silenced.

4. When I remember that God does know me as I am,

____ I feel free to be myself.

____ I worry less.

____ I worry more.

____ I feel anxious.

____ I avoid thinking about this.

5. Jesus's promise, "The water that I give will become in you a fountain of water springing up to eternal life," makes me

____ wonder about the meaning of all this.

____ feel great--I have experienced this fountain of water within me.

____ express gratitude.

____ feel left out--I don't feel I have this.

____ want to know more--I want this fountain flowing inside me.

____ grateful for Jesus Christ.

The psalmist says, "I am wonderful ... and my soul knows this very well" (based on Psalm 139:14). Many of the people I work with don't believe this. They have become separated from their souls. They have lost their hearts and their hearts' desires. They don't know what they want anymore.

Some of these friends can no longer hear the messages God has to give to us--

- that we are loved by Him
- that we are gifted
- that we are precious
- that we are works of art (just as we are)

When we are too busy, too active, and too consumed with everyday life, these important messages cannot get through to us. And then we fret. We wonder about our own value and significance. We begin to do all that our culture tells us to do to feel important. As we seek the approval of others, *we lose the approval that God has already given us.* We forget to listen to His words first.

When our children were born, they could do only two things: (1) cry; and (2) soil their diapers. At that age, they could do nothing to impress us or give love to us. All they could do was *be.* Their *being* was what we loved. That is what we still love about them. Nothing will change that love.

That is how God feels about us today.

Doing Step Four

I begin honestly listing what I know and discover about myself: my strengths, weaknesses, needs, and behavior.

The Fourth-Step Inventory

"A well-defined person is a mature person," a therapist friend of mine told me recently. "Healthy people know their own boundaries, temperament, talents, and capabilities and then use all these to live more fulfilling lives."

The fourth step calls us back. It challenges us to come back to our own core and soul. It asks us to reflect. It invites us to take inventory by looking at four dimensions of our lives:

1. Where did I come from?
2. Who am I right now?
3. What have I been given?
4. What am I doing with what I have been given?

Each time you complete a part of this inventory, you might like to begin with a prayer like this one.

A Fourth-Step Prayer

Dear Lord Jesus,

I don't want to deceive myself. I want to know who I really am. Even though I am afraid of this knowledge sometimes, I really do want to know myself better. I know I have strengths, weaknesses, and needs. That's the way my life is now. I'm sure that's the way it will always be. Help me to be okay with that.

Help me to believe You love me as I am. Help me to love myself as I am. Help me to love others as they are.

Please give me an understanding of my temperament, gifts, and talents so I may properly use them to have a full life and help others in the process.

Thank You, Lord Jesus.

1. Where did I come from?

My feelings about my home, schools, teachers, and classmates (one-sentence descriptions of the first thing that comes to mind)
Ages 1-5 (For instance, I felt loved and wanted.):

_____

_____

Ages 6-9 (This period of my life is kind of a blank.):

_____

_____

Ages 10-12 (I have good feelings about my uncle who spent a lot of time with me during these years.):

_____

_____

Junior high school (I remember feelings of fear, loneliness, turmoil, self-consciousness.):

_____

_____

Senior high school (I remember searching and being unsettled. I'll never forget my first girlfriend.):

_____

_____

College (fun, adventure, hopefulness):

_____

_____

My first job (feeling insecure, afraid of the future, like it was my "god"):

_____

_____

My profession (a struggle; hopeful; fulfillment—I'm persistent):

_____

_____

Some of the people/things that helped make me the way I am now (My grandparents were always there for me when I came home from school. They listened to me as I described my day). Write about your father, mother, siblings, spouse, children, and other influential family members:

_____

_____

_____

_____

_____

_____

_____

_____

_____

_____

_____

_____

_____

_____

_____

_____

_____

_____

_____

_____

_____

_____

Other important information about who I am now (I feel I am moving closer to what God has given me to do; I can relax more; I have learned a great deal about my own needs.):

_____

_____

_____

_____

_____

_____

_____

_____

There are many other tools available to help you get to know yourself better.

In my experience, the best of these tools is the Arno Temperament Profile, but the best resource is within you--the Holy Spirit. The Holy Spirit will lead you and guide you into all truth. Using the Scriptures as your guide, let God teach you about who you are and where you are in life.

2. Who am I right now?

How do I feel about myself right now (check one or several)?
____   I feel loved as I am.
____   I feel I'm a good person.
____   I feel like I am a bad person.
____   I feel I need to do things faster than others to be loved.
____   I feel I need to be perfect to be loved.

What do I really like (tennis, Chinese food, dogs, children)?

_____

_____

_____

What do I really dislike (cats, my overreaction to people who disagree with me, overdrafts)?

_____

_____

_____

_____

_____

What encourages me most (hugs from members of my family, a phone call from my best friend)?

_____

_____

_____

_____

_____

What discourages me most (my judgmental nature, financial problems)?

_____

_____

_____

My strengths (my health, my positive attitude, my ability to do a variety of things well):

_____

_____

_____

_____

_____

My weaknesses (I am too idealistic; I cannot do accounting; I am not a good administrator.):

_____

_____

_____

_____

Some things I like about my body (I am capable of working out; I like my weight; I feel attractive.):

_____

_____

_____

_____

_____

Some things I like about my mind and the way I think (I can think on my feet; I am quick.):

_____

_____

_____

_____

Some things I like about my temperament (I like to reach out to touch others; I like how friendly I can be.):

_____

_____

_____

_____

Some things I can really do well (ski, tennis, sing, dance, swim, talk to strangers, give presentations):

_____

_____

_____

_____

A few things I know I'm *not* good at (supervising others, major construction projects):

_____

_____

_____

_____

_____

What I feel I want to do with my life in the future (keep doing what I'm doing, change my career, plan for retirement):

_____

_____

_____

_____

_____

3. What have I been given?

We have all been given the gift of life. Listed below are passages that describe other specific gifts that have been given to us. Quickly glance through this list and especially notice the italicized words that describe what we have been given.

> *If anyone is in Christ, that person is a new creation. The old has passed away and the new has come.*
> —based on 2 Corinthians 5:17

> *God loved the world so much that He gave His only Son so that everyone who believes in Him will not be lost but have eternal life.*
> —based on John 3:16

> *If you make my word your home, you will indeed be My disciples, you will learn the truth and the truth will make you free. If the Son sets you free, you will be free indeed.*
> —based on John 8:32, 35

There is no condemnation for those who are in Christ Jesus.
—based on Romans 8:1

Blessed be the God and Father of our Lord Jesus Christ who has blessed us with all the spiritual blessings of heaven in Christ. Before the world was made, He chose us in Christ, to be holy and spotless and to live in His presence. We have become His adopted sons and daughters, chosen from the beginning, through Jesus Christ, for His own kind purposes. He gives us freedom and the forgiveness of our sins. He has let us know the mystery of His purpose ... that He will bring everything together under Christ. We have heard the message of the truth and the good news of our salvation and have believed it. We have been given the faith to put our hope in Christ and we have been stamped with the seal of the Holy Spirit.
—based on Ephesians 1:3–14

You are gifted

Paul tells us that each person is given a *gift for the good of all* (based on 1 Corinthians 12:7). Please read through the list of spiritual gifts below. Indicate which of these gifts you know you have been given. Put a question mark by those you think you might have but are not certain of.

____ The gift of God's love
____ The gift of Jesus Christ
____ The gift of eternal life
____ The gift of the Bible
____ The gift of gathering with other believers
____ The gift of the Holy Spirit
____ The gift of the fruits of the Holy Spirit
____ The gift of being a leader
____ The gift of being a prophet
____ The gift of telling others about God

___ The gift of being a pastor
___ The gift of being a teacher
___ The gift of wisdom
___ The gift of knowledge
___ The gift of faith
___ The gift of healing
___ The gift of miraculous powers
___ The gift of discernment
___ The gift of speaking/praying in an unknown "prayer language" (tongues)
___ The gift of helping others
___ The gift of administration
___ The gift of ministering to others
___ The gift of preaching
___ The gift of exhortation
___ The gift of alms-giving
___ The gift of mercy

As part of your prayer and meditation time this week, read the following paraphrases:

> *You, Oh God, created every part of me. You put me together in my mother's womb. I praise You because You are to be feared. Everything You do is strange and wonderful. I know it with all my heart.*
>
> *When my bones were being formed and carefully put together in my mother's womb, when I was growing there in secret, You knew I was there; You saw me before I was born. The days given to me had all been recorded in Your book before any of them ever began.*
>
> —based on Psalm 139:13–16

> *We are God's work of art, created in Jesus Christ.*
>
> —based on Ephesians 2:10

4. What am I doing with what I have been given?

Am I using my gifts?

＿＿ yes ＿＿ no

Am I aware of my weaknesses?

＿＿ yes ＿＿ no

List the weaknesses (letting go, not doing everything perfectly, getting more organized, moving beyond procrastination, facing my issues):

＿＿＿＿＿＿＿＿＿＿＿＿＿＿＿＿＿＿＿＿＿＿＿＿＿＿＿

＿＿＿＿＿＿＿＿＿＿＿＿＿＿＿＿＿＿＿＿＿＿＿＿＿＿＿

Parts of my life that are sinful and need forgiveness (such as my judgmental nature, my lack of trust in God, worrying, my resentful thoughts, my criticism of others):

＿＿＿＿＿＿＿＿＿＿＿＿＿＿＿＿＿＿＿＿＿＿＿＿＿＿＿

＿＿＿＿＿＿＿＿＿＿＿＿＿＿＿＿＿＿＿＿＿＿＿＿＿＿＿

What I am doing that I should not be doing (working in the wrong job, going to movies that influence me negatively, stuffing my feelings rather than sharing them openly with my spouse):

＿＿＿＿＿＿＿＿＿＿＿＿＿＿＿＿＿＿＿＿＿＿＿＿＿＿＿

＿＿＿＿＿＿＿＿＿＿＿＿＿＿＿＿＿＿＿＿＿＿＿＿＿＿＿

＿＿＿＿＿＿＿＿＿＿＿＿＿＿＿＿＿＿＿＿＿＿＿＿＿＿＿

What I am addicted to right now (TV, sexual fantasies, food):

＿＿＿＿＿＿＿＿＿＿＿＿＿＿＿＿＿＿＿＿＿＿＿＿＿＿＿

＿＿＿＿＿＿＿＿＿＿＿＿＿＿＿＿＿＿＿＿＿＿＿＿＿＿＿

＿＿＿＿＿＿＿＿＿＿＿＿＿＿＿＿＿＿＿＿＿＿＿＿＿＿＿

Making Step Four My Own

This section provides you with a format for integrating your feelings, responses to questions, and what you learned from this step, the Scriptures, and in your group meetings.

Date, day, and time of your writings: _____

1. At this point in my life, the major area that I am working on (For instance, getting to know myself better by spending time once each week to reflect on who I am and then making notes in this book.):

_____

_____

2. Major insights I was given into my life through this step (How important it is for me to know my weaknesses and not be afraid to face them):

_____

_____

_____

_____

3. The strongest feeling I have had as I have worked this step (The joy of rediscovering parts of myself—gifts I had forgotten I have):

_____

4. The action I feel called to take as a result of working this step (I will spend time each week thinking about who I am and adding my discoveries to the lists I began in Step Four.):

_____

Chapter 5

FREE AT

LAST

Step Five:

I am ready to honestly share

---

with God and another

---

person the exact nature of

---

my strengths, weaknesses,

---

and behavior.

A very influential counselor/leader told me recently he is convinced that most adults want two major things to happen in their lifetime: (1) They want to be known for who they really are; (2) they want to know another for who that person really is.

Do you think this is true? Is this the way it is for you?

Step Five gives me permission to honestly share the real me with God and another person. This means I am willing to let the other person see my strengths as well as my weaknesses. I allow God and that other person(s) to know my behavior, without defending or explaining it. This can be an extremely difficult step to get started with. We all want this, yet we are all afraid of it.

Step Five can be the most freeing of all the steps. God wants us to be free and whole. Secrets, schizophrenic behavior, denial, partial truths, and unresolved "business" from our past keep us in bondage and slavery. Sin or a secret activity will keep us in darkness. God wants us to be free, to live in the light. Jesus came to bring us freedom.

Letting others know our purpose for life, our course for life, brings them, and us, great freedom. People enjoy the enthusiasm that "focused" people have.

One of the pathways to that freedom, I believe, is to have a sincere conversation with Jesus. A suggestion would be to take the written work you did in your fourth-step inventory and bring it to Him. This could be an extended time on a long walk or a long visit in a chapel. Maybe a weekend at a retreat center would work for you. It could be a time of extended conversation with Jesus about who you are and what you have done. He is faithful; He will forgive us. He is there to affirm us. He will guide us into the future. It is always best to retreat before moving forward.

It may be time, too, to do the same with a close friend or pastor. We are all aware of the need to do spring cleaning in our homes. The same must be done in our souls. By making an appointment with that person, we are doing spring cleaning in our lives.

Years ago, Catholics had an exercise called General Confession. At several intervals in life, a person was asked to review his or her life up to that point. After doing this assessment, the person was to go to a pastor and share his/her life story.

There were several reasons for this General Confession:

1. It gave the person permission to check out how he or she was doing in his or her relationship with God and others.
2. It gave the person the platform to share what he or she had discovered with another person.
3. It helped the person see his or her need for Jesus Christ and His forgiveness.
4. It gave the person some feedback about his or her lifestyle. It encouraged him or her and affirmed his or her humanness.
5. It gave the person an opportunity to confess to God and another person the unconfessed sins of the past. It gave that person the hope of a new beginning.

This General Confession was a great practice. It has long been lost in the shuffle. Step Five brings the concept back in a new way. It provides a way for all of us to experience the freedom and joy of being honest with ourselves, God, and another person.

My best friends are those who know me best. They know my strengths, my weaknesses, and all the peculiar characteristics of my behavior.

A close friend of mine had known about the steps for years. She was afraid of doing the fourth and fifth steps. It took her many years to get up enough courage to begin Step Four and then another year before she could actually go to someone and do Step Five.

"At first I didn't think it was right to go to anyone with this information about myself," she said. "*Why would anyone want to listen to my story?* I had often thought to myself. But then I realized it wasn't my responsibility to be concerned about them. I needed to go and get this stuff out of my system so that I could become a healthier person.

"It's the best thing I've ever done for myself. I feel liberated in knowing that at least one other person knows me and accepts me for who I am."

What the Bible says about Step Five

I am ready to honestly share with God and another person the exact nature of my strengths, weaknesses, and behavior.

Before you talk to another person about your Step Four inventory, think about the truth of the Scriptures below:

1. Jesus was confronted by the Pharisees for eating with tax collectors and sinners. In response to their challenge, Jesus said, *"Those who are well have no need of a physician, but those who are sick. I did not come to call the righteous, but sinners, to repentance"* (Mark 2:17).

Choose from the following:
___ I have always known that Jesus came for sinners, but never believed it.
___ This is hard to believe, really.
___ Jesus came for me. I know I am a sinner. I need Him.
___ This amazes me. Why would Jesus come for sinners or the unhealthy?

2. In his first letter, John writes to the early Christians to lay out the cards: *If we say we have no sin in us, we are deceiving ourselves and refusing to admit the truth; but if we admit to our sins, then God who is faithful and just will forgive us our sins ... but to say that we have never sinned is to call God a liar* (based on 1 John 1:8–10).

Choose from the following:

____ I know I am a sinner, but I don't admit it.

____ I admit I am a sinner in a general sense. I don't think of specific sins when I confess my sins in church or to a friend.

____ I don't know what sin is.

3. In His conversation with Nicodemus, a leading Jew who came to see Jesus at night, Jesus set the record straight about who He was and what His purpose in coming was: *"For God did not send His Son into the world to condemn the world, but that the world through Him might be saved"* (John 3:17).

____ God has sent Jesus to save me, not condemn me. I now believe this is the truth regardless of how I have previously thought about Him.

____ I want to confess my sins and be forgiven.

____ I often feel condemned. This passage is good news for me. I want to believe that Jesus came to save me.

4. The psalmist was a great psychologist. His advice was clear and practical--don't stuff your feelings or your sin:

> *Blessed is he whose sins are forgiven, whose sins are covered. ... When I kept silent, my bones wasted away through my groaning all day long. For day and night Your hand was heavy upon me; my strength was sapped as in the heat of summer. Then I acknowledged my sin to You and did not cover up my iniquity. I said, "I will confess my transgressions to the LORD"-- and You forgave the guilt of my sin.*
>
> —based on Psalm 32:3–5

Psalm 32 shows us that when we hold our sin inside and do not confess it to God, we suffer greatly. We feel emotionally bound up and stuck. We find freedom in confessing our sin. Is there a time when you confessed what you had done to someone else?

    ___   yes   ___   no

Did you find relief?

    ___   yes   ___   no

5. King Solomon's advice in this proverb below is an important element of the fifth step. Sin cannot be covered over. There will always be consequences:

> He who covers his sins will not prosper,
> But whoever confesses and forsakes them will have mercy.
> —Proverbs 28:13

___   I know that stuffing (hiding) my sins is not healthy.
___   I know that as I confess my sins I will find mercy.
___   Confession is the right thing to do. I will do it. I will confess specific sins.

6. James, the author of the Epistle of James, lays out some practical suggestions to the early Christian church. In his "sermon" he makes it clear that we need to *get into the habit of admitting our sins to each other and praying for each other* (based on James 5:16).

Choose the one that best describes how you feel:
___   I am afraid to do this. I don't know why, but I am.
___   I would love to do this, but I don't know how.
___   This sounds like a good idea, but I am not ready yet.

7. Jesus gave a direct challenge to His audience about the use of their gifts. His words had a ring of urgency: *"People don't light a lamp and then hide it or put it under a bowl; instead, they put it on the*

lamp stand so that others may see the light as they come in" (based on Luke 11:33–34).

____ It's really hard for me to tell people about my good qualities or talents. I feel arrogant when I do that.

____ I want to share myself, my history, and my gifts with other people.

____ I am eager to put my "light" out for others to see.

After reading through these Scriptures, you can probably see that God knew that each of us would sin (fall short of His desire for us) and therefore He wrote a process like Step Five into the Scriptures so we could be forgiven and released from the guilt and shame that result from sinful behavior.

Step Five is a natural part of the spiritual process. How do you feel about it now?

I'm most anxious about sharing myself honestly with

____ God.

____ another person.

____ myself.

In sharing myself with another person, I'm afraid of

____ being criticized.

____ being condemned.

____ being known for who I really am.

____ being rejected.

____ being judged.

When you have really tried to let someone else know the real you, what has been your experience?

_____

_____

Making Step Five My Own

This section provides you with a format for integrating your feelings, responses to questions, and what you learned from this step, the Scriptures, and in your group meetings.

Date, day, and time of your writings: _____

1. At this point in my life, the major area that I am working on (For instance, being more conscious of my sins and confessing them as soon as they are brought to mind.):

_____

_____

2. Major insights I was given into my life through this step (How important it is for me to share myself with another person):

_____

_____

_____

_____

3. The strongest feeling I have had as I have worked this step (Anxiety—because I know I am not good at sharing with others):

_____

4. The action I feel called to take as a result of working this step (Go to share with another—that's why I feel anxious):

_____

Chapter 6

READY

Step Six:

I am entirely ready to

---

have Jesus Christ

---

heal all those areas

---

of my life that need

His touch.

Almost everyone I have worked with in a counseling context has needed healing. Most are unaware of what kind of healing they need. Healing comes when we become more aware of our need for it.

Many discover healing needs by doing Steps Four and Five. It is always best if we take care of our needs for healing when we choose to do it, in seasons of our life when we are healthiest.

Step Six invites us to deliberately, gently investigate if there are any of our needs that are unresolved. Any area of our life that is an open file has the capability of affecting every aspect of our lives in a negative way, especially our relationships with those closest to us.

In some cases, unresolved issues can lead to passive aggressive behavior. For example, a sarcastic comment can emerge, be spoken and addressed to someone who is the unintended recipient of our lashing out.

Lack of closure and unfinished business can create barriers and close channels between our heads and hearts, our subconscious and conscious minds, and of course, in our interpersonal relationships.

Unhealed, unaddressed needs in our past prevent us from moving freely into the future.

Unfortunately, many of our attempts to get healing are futile because they deal only with the symptoms. Most of the pain in our lives is a result of unmet needs. When we do a temperament analysis, we discover we all have non-negotiable needs that must be met. These non-negotiable needs are very specific and personal. It is essential that we know what these needs are and that we respect ourselves enough to be sure these needs are met in appropriate ways.

Getting our needs met brings life-giving nourishment. We are energized through getting these needs met. Life is rich, full, complete, and we flourish when these needs are met. Our creativity comes to life. St. Ignatius said, "The glory of God is His people fully alive."

When we are not nourished and our needs are not met, we are disappointed, discouraged, and in pain. We have many symptoms, like depression, anxiety, loneliness, insecurities, fears, rejection, fatigue, emotional wounds. The behaviors that usually accompany these symptoms include irritability, sarcasm, passive aggressiveness, anger, resentment, and impatience. The core reason for symptoms and these behaviors must be addressed. Trying hard to be less irritable when one of your major needs is not met is much like telling a person who has not had anything to eat for a week that life will get better for him someday.

The temperament process clearly defines the specific needs each of us have and helps us understand how to get those needs met. The temperament process also helps us understand the needs that have not been met in our lives to this point. It's these unmet needs that trigger negative symptoms. It's these unmet needs that must be discovered for healing to take place. Jesus is able and willing to meet these needs.

A very successful attorney had been coming to meetings because she felt she was addicted to relationships. She said she had an empty spot in her life, and she didn't feel good about herself.

For many years, she had known she didn't get along well with people. She had no close friends. Once in a while she developed a friendship with someone, but the friendship would be "sabotaged," as she put it, by her own "crazy" behavior. While she felt she was inviting the person to come closer, she was at the same time pushing her friend away.

Though she wanted intimacy, she did things to avoid it. Whenever anyone got close to her, she did something to make the relationship undesirable for the other person.

This fear of intimacy showed up in her marriage relationship as well. Though her marriage had no major problems, on the surface, it had little joy. Her husband had resigned himself to having a fairly platonic relationship with his wife. It was not what he wanted, but he felt helpless and hopeless. He moved into a mode of "doing his own thing" while she did hers.

At age thirty-eight, this woman watched her thirteen-year marriage dissipate. Her husband was becoming more demanding. She wanted to meet his needs but did not know how to do it. She had withdrawn into herself more than ever.

Hope came to her when she began attending a group that was working on the material in this book. The critical circumstances in her life compelled her to find some answers.

Unfortunately, we are always driven by pain. We hear better and listen more when we are suffering. This woman had to face the facts. She was unhappy. She was contributing to her husband's unhappiness.

"Why am I living life like this? Why do I do this? What makes me want to be close to people and then push them away when they come close?" she asked in one of the group meetings.

She had taken an important step toward recovery. She was owning her temperament, personality, and behavior. She was admitting to who she really is. She was ready, through the painful circumstances of her life, to make some needed changes.

"I wasn't ready six months ago. I have had several crises in my life, but none of them has been major enough to make me want to change. Now, I want to change. I know I have to change," she said. "I am disgusted with my own life. Something has to give. I need to do something before I lose my husband and family." And the sixth step helped her change.

In doing a temperament analysis for her and her husband, we discovered she had a very high (non-negotiable) need for affection. Her parents were not affectionate. Her father was very distant, seldom expressing any affection to his wife or daughter.

For most of her life, her needs for feedback, encouragement, affirmation, tenderness, and closeness had not been met by anyone. Most of her attempts to reach out and get those needs met ended in disappointment. The repeated disappointment convinced her that her affectionate needs would never get met. And that lack of hope fueled her disillusionment and fear of relationships.

In her college and law school years, she had become desperate and looked for affectionate fulfillment in a number of inappropriate relationships with men. These relationships deepened her wound.

The sixth step helped her identify the source of her pain and behavior and motivated her to get the help she needed. Her husband, at the same time, became aware of his own needs and grew in his desire to learn more about her needs.

In addition to the counseling work that the three of us did, I suggested they read several chapters from Gospel of Luke. Luke was a physician, and so his gospel has several stories of how Jesus healed people who needed His touch.

One particular story made a great deal of sense to them. That story and the following exercises helped them identify their needs and the fact that Jesus could heal her.

What the Bible says about Step Six

One Sabbath day Jesus was teaching in one of the synagogues, and a woman was there who had been ill for eighteen years. She had a spirit of weakness. She was bent over double and was unable to straighten up properly. She could not hold her head erect.

This woman stepped into Jesus's life out of nowhere. Little was known about her then. Little is known about her to this day. No one seemed to know for sure what her problem was. They felt sorry for her and felt helpless but simply accepted this posture as normal for her.

When Jesus noticed her, He called her and said, "You are set free from your illness!" And He put His hands upon her, and at once she stood upright and praised God.

Jesus must have known the private agony this woman had gone through because of her illness. He knew her need for healing. He touched her and set her free immediately (based on Luke 13:10–13).

1. Check the statements that are true about this woman:
    ____   She was unable to straighten up.
    ____   Jesus came to her home.
    ____   Jesus told her she would be set free from her illness.
    ____   She praised God.

2. Check the statements that are true about you:
    ____   I have a pain/problem that has been with me for a long time.
    ____   I am entirely ready to have Jesus touch me and make my life different.
    ____   I want to be entirely ready, but I don't know how.
    ____   Ready for what? I don't understand.

3. When Jesus says, "You are free from your illness," he means
    ____   "Find a way to straighten up and then I'll help you with your illness."
    ____   What He says.
    ____   He touched and healed her because He loved her, and He didn't expect anything in return from her.

Doing Step Six

I asked the successful attorney to think about the areas in which she needed Jesus's healing touch. She was very willing. Would you be willing to do the same?

1. Area(s) of your life in which you most need healing today:
    ____   Physical (For instance, I need help in getting more exercise, in watching what I eat more carefully, with my neck ache.):

    _____

    ____   Mental (I do not feel very stable mentally right now. I feel bogged down and out of balance.)

    _____

___ Emotional (I feel drained or numb. I don't have anything to give to anyone else.):

_____

___ Spiritual (I try hard to have more intimacy with God, but God seems so far away. I don't devote any time at all to my relationship with God and I want this to change.):

_____

___ Relational (I am having a terrible time communicating with my husband. I have not spoken to my brother in five years.):

_____

2. In order to have these areas of my life healed I need:
    ___ to have more pain--I don't hurt enough yet.
    ___ time and some solitude to sort things out.
    ___ to go back to Steps Four and Five for a while longer
    ___ nothing. I am ready and eager.

3. Believing in Jesus Christ and His power to touch and heal me is:
    ___ very difficult for me. I don't feel worthy of His healing touch.
    ___ frightening. That's getting too close for me.
    ___ farfetched. Jesus doesn't do that kind of thing anymore.
    ___ very easy. I've experienced His healing touch and power before.
    ___ I have little doubt about Jesus and His power to heal.

Finally, I suggested that the attorney read the following encouraging story from the Scriptures to see if she could find herself in it.

Jesus went back to Cana in Galilee where He had miraculously changed the water into wine. There was an important court official there whose son was sick at Capernaum. Hearing that Jesus had arrived in Galilee, the official went and pleaded with Him to come to Capernaum and cure his son, who was at the point of death.

Jesus said, "Go home. Your son will live." The man believed what Jesus had said and started on his way; and while he was still on the journey back, his servants met him with the news that his boy was alive. He asked them when the boy had begun to recover. "The fever left him yesterday," they said, "at about one o'clock." The father realized that this was exactly the time when Jesus had said, "Your son will live."

He and all his household believed in Jesus.

—based on John 4:46–54

1. From everything I can gather from this reading, the court official was:

____ desperate to have his son healed.

____ ready to do anything Jesus suggested.

____ entirely ready for Jesus to intervene in the life of his son.

2. What is most impressive to me about this true story is:

____ the faith of the court official. When Jesus told him to go home, he believed and started on his way.

____ the fact that Jesus healed the man's son from a distance. He did not need to be present for the son to be healed.

____ the healing Jesus did.

3. The most important thing I've learned about Jesus through this reading is:

___ His word is good. When He said, "Go home. Your son will live," the court official could believe what He said and act on it.

___ Jesus's power to heal.

___ the authority Jesus has. When He says something, it happens.

___ how timely His intervention was.

___ Jesus is capable of healing all those areas of our lives that need His touch. I believe He is waiting for me to come to Him, as the court official did.

4. The most important thing I've learned about myself through this reading is:

___ I need healing. I'm ready.

___ I believe Jesus can heal me.

___ if Jesus tells me to do something, I will do it without hesitation.

___ I need more time to think about all of this.

Making Step Six My Own

This section provides you with a format for integrating your feelings, responses to questions, and what you learned from this step, the Scriptures, and in your group meetings.

Date, day, and time of your writings: _____

1. At this point in my life, the major area that I am working on (For instance, I am working on letting Jesus heal me emotionally.):

_____

_____

2. Major insights I was given into my life through this step (Until I looked at this step, I didn't realize how much I need God's healing.):

_____

_____

_____

_____

3. The strongest feeling I have had as I have worked this step (Hope that I can someday become a whole person):

_____

4. The action I feel called to take as a result of working this step (Pray more and receive God's blessings):

_____

Chapter 7

ASKING FOR

HEALING

Step Seven:

I humbly ask Jesus

Christ to change my

weaknesses into

strengths so I will

become more like Him.

God is touching me. He is healing me. He is moving me toward a freer, more accepting, and more Spirit-led lifestyle. He is transforming my judgmentalism into healthy intuition.

When I was younger, I felt I couldn't come to God until I had a better, cleaner life. I avoided some people because I hadn't done enough work on improving myself to be ready to present myself to them. I had given myself a message: "You're not good enough as you are; you're inadequate; work on yourself; shape up some more so you can be acceptable to God and others."

Perfectionism is bondage to self-imposed standards, family messages, and cultural values. God is delivering me from this bondage into His great freedom. One of the ways He does it is through Scripture.

Paul asked a hard question in his letter to the Colossians. "If you have really died with Christ to the principles of this world, why do you still let its rules dictate to you, as though you were still living in the world?" (based on Colossians 2:20).

In his letter to the Galatians he says, "When Christ freed us, He meant us to stay free. Stand firm then and do not submit again to the yoke of slavery" (based on Galatians 5:1). And in his letter to the Romans he wrote, "Don't let the world squeeze you into its mold, but let God remold your minds from within" (based on Romans 12:2).

How can we do this? How can we be set free from the squeeze of perfectionism and other cultural pressures? Step Seven gives us the answer--humbly ask Jesus Christ to change our weaknesses into strengths. We can ask with confidence, not because we want something just for ourselves, but because our sincere desire is to become more like Him.

Paul says in Colossians 3:1-3 to look for the things that are in heaven, where Christ is, sitting at God's right hand. This is where our eyes should be focused--not on ourselves, not on our problems, not on our way of doing things.

Another area where God has been doing significant healing in my life is in my workaholism. Workaholism is a symptom of a performance-based mentality. My value comes through what I do, accomplish, own, or control, this mentality says. My identity is based on these externals, not on who I am.

From God's perspective, the opposite is true. God looks at the heart. He looks at character. He wants us to become more like Jesus Christ. Jesus Christ is not a driven, performance-based person. From everything I can gather in my reading of the New Testament, He was never in a hurry. He had no great earthly plans. His life was simple. He had one purpose in life––to die on the cross for our sins so that He could save us.

Performance-based identity or grace-based identity––we can choose. The world has us convinced that performance is all that matters and that grace is meaningless. I need to be healed from this way of thinking. I humbly ask Jesus to change this part of me.

Ultimately all that counts is whether we have loved––as Jesus loves. Have I allowed Him to love me? Have I allowed Him to use me as a vessel to love and serve others? Have I loved Him, myself, my spouse, my family, my neighbor? Nothing else matters in comparison. Only love counts.

What about you?

Jesus can change all dimensions of our lives. We, however, have a part to play in the process. Our part is to be honest and identify our weaknesses, then humbly ask for His help. The rest is up to Him. He will respond in His own way and time. He encourages us to ask and seek. His promise is that "if anyone thirsts, let that person come to Me and drink." Jesus will help us.

What are your greatest areas of weakness right now? Check the statements that apply to you.

_____ I tend to criticize others.

_____ I sometimes lie to defend myself.

_____ I tend to dislike people who have different beliefs than I do or who come from different backgrounds.

_____ I tend to judge people quickly.

_____ I sometimes want to do things I know are wrong.

_____ Sometimes I am attracted to a person other than my spouse.

_____ I tend to envy my neighbors or others at work when something good happens to them.

_____ _____

Are you willing to humbly ask Jesus Christ to change those weaknesses into strengths? Do you sincerely desire to become more like Christ?

To become more like Christ, we need to be aware of, identify, and deal with our weaknesses.

Every person has strengths. Every person has weaknesses. Jesus Christ can change our weaknesses into strengths.

Step Six reminds us of how disgusting our behavior can sometimes be. Step Seven helps us realize the hope we have in Jesus Christ––that He can take these weak areas of our lives and make them into strengths.

What is it that you want Jesus to heal for you right now (for instance, my relationship with a friend, my headaches, my lack of trust, a bad experience in my past)?

_____

As I read the letters from the apostle Paul, I am amazed at how much he went through. He was one of the greatest leaders history has ever known. Like all great leaders, he had enemies, great struggles, and personal issues to deal with. In the passage below, he describes one of these as the "thorn in his side." He says this thorn was given to him so that he might not become proud.

No one is really sure what that thorn was, but his own testimony says that this weakness ended up being a strength for Paul:

> To keep me from becoming conceited because of these surpassingly great revelations, there was given me a thorn in my flesh, a messenger of Satan, to torment me. Three times I pleaded with the Lord to take it away from me. But He said to me, "My grace is sufficient for you, for my power is made perfect in weakness." Therefore I will boast all the more gladly about my weaknesses so that Christ's power may rest on me. That is why, for Christ's sake, I delight in weaknesses, in insults, in hardships, in persecutions, in difficulties. For when I am weak, then I am strong.
>
> —based on 2 Corinthians 12:7–10

After reading this passage I:

____ understand better why some people might be given "thorns."

____ understand better why God might not answer some of my prayers (that it's best for me to have "thorns" in my life to keep me humble).

____ believe God's grace is sufficient and His power is made perfect in weakness.

Jesus changes the life of one man

Jesus went up to a Jewish festival in Jerusalem. At the Sheep Pool in Jerusalem, there is a building with five covered porches surrounding it. Under these porches were crowds of sick, lame, blind, and paralyzed people. They were all there waiting for the water to move, for at intervals the angel of the Lord came down into the pool and the water was disturbed. The first person to enter the water after this disturbance was cured of any ailment that person suffered.

One man there had an illness that had lasted thirty-eight years, and when Jesus saw him lying there and knew he had been in this condition for a long time, He said, "Do you want to be healed?"

"I can't," the sick man said, "for I have no one to help me into the pool at the movement of the water. While I'm trying to get there, someone else always gets in ahead of me."

Jesus told him, "Stand up, roll up your sleeping mat, and go home!" Instantly the man was healed. He rolled up his mat and began walking (based on John 5:1–9).

Think about this miraculous healing with me.

1. Which best describes the man at the pool?
___ He was persistent; he must have sincerely sought healing.
___ He was psychologically sick, not physically sick.
___ He was extremely ill; that's why Jesus singled him out.
___ He deserved Jesus's help after waiting for thirty-eight years.
___ It's hard to know much about this person from this reading.

2. In what ways are you like the man at the pool?
___ I am physically sick.
___ I am psychologically sick.
___ I am holding on to things inside that make me feel sick sometimes.
___ I want to be healed.
___ I have gone to the "place of healing" many times and nothing has happened to me.

3. When Jesus asked the man at the pool if he wanted to become whole, He was asking him:
___ if he wanted to become healthy physically.
___ if he wanted to become healthy psychologically.

___ if he wanted to become spiritually healthy.

___ if he wanted his whole life to be integrated, sound, and healthy.

___ if he wanted things to stay the way they were.

4. When Jesus asks you if you want to become whole, how do you answer?

___ Not yet--I'm not ready.

___ I don't know.

___ I'm ready to become whole. What is my part in the process?

___ I really like my life the way it is, even though parts of it are unhealthy.

___ Please come, Lord Jesus, and make me whole.

5. What strikes me most about this passage is:

___ the fact that Jesus came to touch one person in that crowd.

___ Jesus's offer to make the man whole.

___ the power Jesus has to make whole.

___ the offer I feel Jesus is making to me.

___ the fact that Jesus would even bother spending time with an insignificant person like this man.

Doing Step Seven

Now that you know the power Jesus has to change your weaknesses into strengths, think again about Step Seven: I humbly ask Jesus Christ to change my weaknesses into strengths so that I will become more like Him.

Step Seven says, "I humbly ask Jesus Christ ..."

___ It is hard for me to ask anyone for anything. I can do all things on my own.

___ Asking doesn't pay. I've tried. It just hasn't worked for me.

___ Jesus doesn't have time for me and my petty problems. Why bother asking Him for help?

___ I have asked. He is responding.

___ I have asked. He has responded!

Step Seven says, "I humbly ask Jesus Christ to change my weaknesses into strengths."

___ I believe He can do this, but I'm not sure I want it done.

___ I still don't know my weaknesses.

___ I have experienced this. Jesus has and is changing my weaknesses into strengths. Praise Him!

Step Seven says, "I humbly ask Jesus Christ to change my weaknesses into strengths so I will become more like Him."

___ I want to become more like Jesus.

___ I want to become more like Jesus but am doubtful it could ever happen.

___ I would give anything (everything) to become more like Christ.

___ I know I have become more like Him in at least a few small ways.

Making Step Seven My Own

This section provides you with a format for integrating your feelings, responses to questions, and what you learned from this step, the Scriptures, and in your group meetings.

Date, day, and time of your writings: _____

1. At this point in my life, the major area that I am working on (For instance, I am humbly asking Jesus and others for what I need.):

_____

_____

2. Major insights I was given into my life through this step (I am ready to have Jesus heal me.):

_____

_____

_____

_____

3. The strongest feeling I have had as I have worked this step (Humility—I realize that I need to be more honest about my "humaness")

_____

4. The action I feel called to take as a result of working this step (Ask for help.):

_____

Chapter 8

SHARING THE

HEALING

Step Eight:

I make a list of the

people I have hurt and

become willing to go

to them to mend the

relationship.

When everything else is gone, relationships will stand. Nothing is as important as our family and friends. Most families have a history of broken relationships and have forgotten how broken they are. When one person in the family begins to deal with this brokenness, relationships within the family can improve, but not without cost or pain.

The relationships we have, we need to keep. Some of the ones we have lost, we need to work to restore.

Step Eight simplifies the process of reuniting with someone we have been alienated from. The step asks us to do two things:

1: Make a list of those we have offended, abused, violated, ignored, neglected—those we have hurt in any way. Some people, some temperaments, are completely unaware they have done anything to offend anyone. It will be very difficult for them to make such a list.

2: The second part of Step Eight asks us to make a list of those who have offended us. Our natural response to those who have hurt us is to avoid them and try to forget what they have done to harm us. Time does not heal. Dealing with the relationship does.

Step Eight has a "sting" to it. Who wants to open the door to history of hurt?

This is a door that must be opened. Any unresolved relationship issues are like open wounds in our hearts, minds and souls.

Closure is required. *Closure brings healing and changes wounds into scars.* Scars don't hurt—they are only reminders of something that happened in the past. Wounds are like open reservoirs in our minds that are filled with mostly unresolved experiences. A simple word from another person, a "tone" or a glance, can trigger an inappropriate, disproportionate response to the situation. This naive, innocent input from the other person can set off a chain reaction of overwhelming, out of control behavior without us knowing where that intensity came from.

Behavior is almost always symptomatic, a reaction to something immediate. But behavior has deep roots. Addressing the behavior (symptoms) without addressing the roots (core issues, reasons for the reactions) will ultimately lead to more frustration and repeated bad behavior.

The reservoir needs to be drained. The wound needs to be healed. The relationship needs to be reconciled. Only Jesus has the ability to do any and all of these. Without Him and His willingness to help, we are left to our own insufficient, inadequate, resources.

He is willing. He is able. The Scriptures are filled with promises, stories and reminders that Jesus Christ has done and will continue to do the impossible. For more than forty years, I have heard hundreds (thousands?) of stories of His intervention, His doing the impossible, His touching hard hearts and changing lives.

He came to die for us to reconcile us to His Father. He wants us to be reconciled to others. He is the Prince of Peace. He is driven to make peace. He is hurt by division and separation and is longing to step in to restore and redeem "brokenness."

How can restoration happen?

1. We admit to our powerlessness over the situation.
2. We acknowledge that God is powerful, that all things are possible for Him.
3. We surrender and be willing to do whatever He asks us to do.
4. We claim/own what our part was/is in the demolition of the relationship.
5. We are postured to take the initiative to go and restore the relationship.
6. With God's help, and following the guidelines of Step Eight, we go with the intention of reconciling the relationship.

Married couples recovering from an affair struggle with closure. The person who had the affair is eager to hastily put it all behind him or her. The "victim spouse" needs much healing, reassurance, and evidence that this will never happen again. Putting closure to the affair is much more difficult for the "victim."

One of the most important words in this step is the word *willing*. If we are willing to let go and let God work in our lives, anything can happen. What seems impossible becomes possible when we are willing.

There are many reasons we might not be willing to do Step Eight, but the benefits will far outweigh the thought and energy we put into preparing for reconciliation.

One of my mentors often reminded me that being at peace with God, ourselves, and others is priceless. The freedom that comes with knowing we no longer hold any grudges, have any resentment, have surrendered our legitimate anger, and have allowed God's grace to flow freely into our hearts is beyond description. There is no better feeling than being released from being held captive by our own unresolved feelings.

In my many years of doing this step process, I have heard and been a part of hundreds of stories of "captives set free" through Step Eight.

There are some very valid reasons why most of us would not be eager to make either list, the list of those we have offended or the list of those who have offended us. Identifying those reasons might help us move on in the process.

Perhaps the main reason for avoiding this step is that we feel like we were right, the other person was wrong. Our pride can keep us from taking steps toward the necessary breakthrough. I have worked with people or groups who have been alienated for many years (decades) because of one disagreement over a very simple matter.

Some feel embarrassed as they think about the frivolous issue that separated them in the first place.

Others feel too hurt to want to go "back there" in their minds. "If I open that door, there is no telling where this will take me. I am afraid and don't want to re-live stuff."

Others, some specific temperaments, live in denial and keep telling themselves that whatever happened was "No big deal. What's the problem?"

Some say, "That happened long ago. It's been forgotten. It doesn't matter." But history matters. Landmark events in our lives have had great power in defining who we are today.

Another reason some people find it difficult to do this step is because they are not yet ready to forgive. In their minds, forgiving means they approve of what happened and they are endorsing whatever the other person did to offend them.

These are all very legitimate reasons to not do this step. We need God's help.

What the Bible says about forgiveness

Please read the following passages and select a response that most describes where you are right now.

Jesus gave His disciples teaching they had never heard before. He spoke with authority. They listened. Perhaps His most difficult teaching was the one that follows. It is an important one as we think about those who have hurt us.

1. Jesus says, "Love your enemies, do good to those who hate you, bless those who curse you, and pray for those who spitefully use you" (Luke 6:27–28).

   ___ Without Your help, Lord Jesus, I cannot go back to those who have hurt me.

   ___ I need to make amends.

   ___ This is impossible for me. I want to do it, but cannot pray for or go to those who mistreated me.

   ___ I can't do this yet, but what I can do is clearly identify those who have hurt me.

2. In response to their expressed desire to pray, Jesus taught the disciples a pattern for prayer. Here is a portion of what is now entitled the Lord's Prayer:

> *Forgive us our debts, as we forgive our debtors.*
> *and do not lead us into temptation, but deliver us from*
> *the evil one.*

After He finished the prayer, Jesus added,

> *For if you forgive men their trespasses, your heavenly*
> *Father will also forgive you. But if you do not forgive men*
> *their trespasses, neither will your Father forgive your*
> *trespasses.*

—Matthew 6:12–13a, 14–15

What is your response to Jesus' prayer:

___ I need God's forgiveness.

___ I need God's help in forgiving others.

___ I know I live dangerously if I do not forgive others.

3. Solomon, a wise Old Testament king, wrote most of the book of Proverbs. One of his important proverbs says, "Do not say, 'I'll pay you back for this wrong!' Wait for the Lord, and He will deliver you. Do not say, 'I'll do to him as he has done to me; I'll pay that person back for what he did'" (based on Proverbs 20:22; 24:29).

___ This passage helps me with my feelings of resentment and revenge. It puts them in perspective.

___ I am learning to let the Lord deliver me.

___ I will let the Lord pay back a person who has wronged me. He will do what is right.

4. Part of loving each other is being sure that the relationship is reconciled and "together." People seek this unity, which is evidence that we are His disciples. Jesus says, "A new commandment I give to you, that you love one another; as I have

93

loved you, that you also love one another. By this all will know that you are My disciples, if you have love for one another" (John 13:34–35).

____ To love my brothers or sisters means I am reconciled with them.

____ If I love them, I will do what I can to make amends.

____ By the love we have for one another, the world will know we are Christ's disciples.

Strange as it may seem, most people begin the work of Step Eight by making amends with themselves. They gently recognize areas of their lives where they have hurt themselves. For some, this means they have been too hard on themselves, expecting too much and depriving themselves of a great deal. For others, it has meant recognizing they have not lived with integrity.

One man shared in a group recently that he has never really done anything for himself. "I felt selfish whenever I bought something for myself. I unnecessarily deprived myself of basic things I need. I have made amends with myself about this. And now, once in a while, I buy myself a treat. I always buy myself a birthday gift."

Most people have at least one unreconciled relationship in their lives. As a person who is in a relationship with Jesus Christ, I know I am loved and forgiven. I have the freedom to love and forgive others. I can take the initiative to mend the relationship even if I am convinced I have not been the one responsible for breaking the relationship.

Reconciliation is the highest priority. In most cases it doesn't even matter who was right or who was wrong. As one of Jesus's disciples I am responsible to make the move to reconcile.

> Lord Jesus, help me to do this step. I resent this person for what he has done to me. I know You want our relationship to be restored. Years have gone by, and we still do not greet one another. This is not

what You want from me or us. Please give me the courage to go to him. Help me to say I'm sorry. Give me the strength to ask his forgiveness. And then give me the faith to entrust all the results to You.

Doing Step Eight

I will make a list of the people I have hurt and become willing to go to them to mend the relationship.

Make your list of people you have harmed. Begin with those you have hurt today. Gradually work your way back in time so that you include those you have hurt this past week, this month, this year. Don't be embarrassed. We have all hurt someone. All of us have failed. All of us have sinned. All of us need this step.

Making the list and being willing to mend these relationships is all we need to do in Step Eight. Step Nine is the action step.

The list of those I have hurt

I acknowledge that I have hurt myself in the following ways:

_____

_____

_____

Family:

_____

_____

_____

_____

Friends:

_____

_____

_____

_____

_____

Relatives:

_____

_____

_____

_____

Teachers:

_____

_____

_____

My supervisors, mentors, pastors, leaders:

_____

_____

_____

Others:

_____

_____

The tax collector who took Step Eight

One man in the Bible gave his life to Jesus (did Step Three) and then felt compelled to make amends (Step Eight) to those he had harmed. His name was Zacchaeus. As a chief tax collector in Jericho he had collected extra taxes so he could make more money.

Zacchaeus discovered that Jesus was making His way through Jericho. He was curious about Jesus and wanted to meet Him. The crowd prevented him from doing so because he was very short. So he ran ahead and climbed up into a sycamore tree to get a view of Jesus as Jesus was heading that way.

When Jesus reached the spot, He looked up and saw the man and said, "Zacchaeus, hurry and come down. I must be your guest today." So Zacchaeus hurriedly climbed down and gladly welcomed Him. But those standing by muttered their disapproval: "Now Jesus has gone to stay with a real sinner."

But Zacchaeus himself stopped and said to the Lord, "Look, sir, I will give half my property to the poor. And if I have cheated anybody out of anything, I will pay him back four times as much."

Jesus said to him, "Salvation has come to this house today. It is the lost that I came to seek and to save" (based on Luke 19:1–10).

1. Why do you think Zacchaeus was so anxious to see Jesus?
___ He had everything else in life, and he needed some excitement.
___ His life was empty.
___ He was fed up with his own lifestyle. He knew it was wrong to cheat others. He knew he needed Jesus's help to change his behavior.

2. Jesus came for the
___ rich and famous.
___ short and funny.
___ lost.
___ religious people.

3. Zacchaeus's first vocal response to Jesus was:
___ I will give half my property to the poor.
___ If I've cheated anybody out of anything, I'll pay him back ten times.
___ I never hurt anybody.
___ I didn't do anything wrong.

4. Imagine for a moment that you are Zacchaeus. You have met Jesus, and He has invited Himself to your house for lunch.

    What was your reaction as He invited Himself?

    How does His visit make you feel?

    Does His presence remind you of the need to make amends (as it reminded Zach)?

    Do you sense Jesus's love for you?

    Do you feel ready to make amends because God has come to visit you and let you know that He accepts you as you are?

Open yourself to be reminded of someone you may have hurt. This is an act of maturity and a necessary part of growth. Maybe it was a lie you told or a rumor you started. Perhaps you slighted someone or insulted a family member or fellow worker. Look again at your list of behaviors in Step Four. Have you done something wrong to another person? The purpose of Step Eight is to get ready to mend the relationship with that person so you can be free.

We do this process because it is the right thing to do right now, at this moment. It will take some courage, but getting it done will be worth it. You will be set free. We all need to be set free, to make amends, to make every effort to clean the slate. We all need the peace and relief that comes with knowing we have done our best to restore our damaged relationships.

To the Lord, relationships were primary. Jesus came to die for us so that our relationship with the Father could be restored. He came to break down the walls between us, God, and others.

We are all familiar with the scriptural text, "If you bring your gift to the altar, and there remember that your brother [sister] has something against you, leave your gift there before the altar, and go … be reconciled to your brother [sister], and then come and offer your gift" (Matthew 5:23–24). Step Eight is another way of reminding us that we need to be reconciled with our brothers and sisters.

My List of Those Who Have Hurt Me

My list of those who have hurt me:

Family:

_____

_____

_____

_____

_____

_____

Friends:

_____

_____

_____

Relatives:

_____

_____

_____

Teachers:

_____

_____

Bosses, supervisors, leaders, pastors:

_____

_____

_____

Others:

_____

_____

_____

Forgiveness is not easy. Without Jesus's help, it is impossible. With God's help, all things are possible. As we will discover in Step Ten, making amends as soon as we know we have done something to offend someone is best and easier. The longer we wait to make amends, the more difficult it becomes.

Making Step Eight My Own

This section provides you with a format for integrating your feelings, responses to questions, and what you learned from this step, the Scriptures, and in your group meetings.

Date, day, and time of your writings: _____

1. At this point in my life, the major area that I am working on (For instance, I am making amends with a former employer.):

_____

_____

2. Major insights I was given into my life through this step (As I forgive, I will be forgiven.):

_____

_____

_____

_____

3. The strongest feeling I have had as I have worked this step (Fear—I am afraid to try to be reconciled.):

_____

4. The action I feel called to take as a result of working this step (I feel I must take the initiative in reconciling with a member of my family.):

_____

Chapter 9

MAKING

AMENDS

Step Nine:

I make amends with

---

the people I have hurt,

---

except when to do

---

so might bring harm

---

to them or others.

It took me many years to prepare to make amends with my father. It took just a few minutes to actually make amends. My temperament is the type that thinks about too many things for too long, and usually says too little too late. I had to decide whether it would be best to go see him and try to make amends— or leave "well enough alone." I decided to go.

Many, many times I rehearsed what I would say to my father. When I finally got the courage to go to be with him, all the rehearsals and all of the wasted time were in vain. He was more ready than I was.

In a few sentences, I told him how much he had hurt me and how much I missed having him as a father. He understood. He agreed and in his own way, he apologized. For the next five years (the last five years of his life) our relationship was good.

I am very grateful for this encounter with my dad. I did it because it was the right thing to do and the timing felt right. Since that experience (now many years ago) I have a better understanding of my dad. I have great and growing compassion for him. I have no resentment, regrets, or anger. I love him very much and look forward to someday soon seeing him in heaven.

Because making amends is a two-way street, I had my own issues and feelings to apologize for. As I reflect on this, I often wish I had spent more time on what I had done to offend him instead of focusing primarily on what he had done to hurt me.

Step Nine is about making a decision about whether going to the person we have hurt or the person who has hurt us to make amends is the right thing to do.

How about you?

To the best of your ability, describe what holds you back from mending the broken relationships in your life:

____ I fear rejection.

____ I am anxious about the response.

____ I am embarrassed about the issues I will need to raise.
____ It's not worth it.
____ It's no big deal. I really don't need to go.

To the best of your ability, describe the benefits you get from keeping your distance from this person(s):

____ It feels safer to keep things as they are.
____ I'm so used to living this way, changing my relationship with this person would be too hard to do.
____ It's become a game to keep dancing around each other; I don't know how to stop the game.
____ I don't know.

The Bible tells the story of one son who had the courage to return to his home to make amends to his father.

The Prodigal Son

Once there was a man who had two sons. The younger one said to his father, "Father, give me my share of the property that will come to me in my inheritance." So the father divided up his property between the two sons. Before very long, the younger son collected all his belongings and went off to a foreign land where he squandered his wealth in wild living.

When he had run through all his money, a terrible famine arose, and he began to feel the pinch. Then he went and hired himself out to one of the citizens of that country, who sent him out into the fields to feed the pigs. He got to the point of longing to stuff himself with pig food, but not a person would offer him anything.

Then he came to his senses and cried aloud, "Dozens of my father's hired men have more food than they can eat, and here I am dying of hunger! I will get up and go back to my father and I will say to him, 'Father, I have done wrong in the sight of heaven and in your eyes. I don't deserve to be called your son any more. Please take me on as one of your hired men.'"

So he got up and went to his father. But while he was still some distance off, his father saw him, and his heart went out to him, and he ran and fell and kissed him on his neck. But his son said, "Father, I have done wrong in the sight of heaven and in your eyes. I don't deserve to be called your son anymore."

"Hurry," called out his father to the servants. "Get the best clothes and put them on him! Put a ring on his finger and shoes on his feet. Get that calf we've fattened and kill it, and we will have a feast and a celebration! For this is my son. I thought he was dead, and he's alive again. I thought I had lost him and he's found!" And they began to get the festivities going (based on Luke 15:11–24).

1. In this story:
   ____ I am like the son, returning to ask forgiveness and to make amends.
   ____ I am like the father, waiting for someone to return to me to make amends.
   ____ I can't relate to this story.
   ____ I see God the Father waiting for me to come back home to Him.

2. The main thing I get out of this story right now is
   ___ don't ask for your inheritance when you are young.
   ___ Jesus is like the father.
   ___ how the father forgave the son and was waiting for him to return.
   ___ I want to go "home" to get things straightened out.

3. The hardest thing about going to make amends for me is
   ___ making up my mind whether I should go.
   ___ making the first move to go.
   ___ going.

4. For just a few moments, put yourself in the shoes of the son who returns home after wasting his inheritance. What are your feelings as you are walking toward your home and you see your father stepping out to meet you?

_____

_____

5. Talk with your group or write about the most important person you need to make amends with. What is your plan for making amends? (You can use the reading of this book as your way to break into the conversation and your need to make amends).

_____

_____

_____

_____

_____

_____

_____

_____

To help you get started in taking Step Nine, think about the list you made in Step Eight. Of this list of people that you have hurt, who do you feel most needs you to make amends with them right now?

Name_____

How was the relationship hurt?

_____

_____

Verbal amend (What will you say?):

_____

_____

Anything else you need to do to prepare for this meeting:

_____

_____

What the Bible says about Step Nine

1. Jesus is talking to His heavenly Father when He says, "I pray that all of them may be one, Father, just as You are in Me and I am in You. May they also be in us so that the world may believe that You have sent Me" (based on John 17:21).

   ___ I know God wants me to be one (united) with my family and friends.

   ___ I believe Jesus has prayed that we would all be one.

   ___ I want to be united with my family and friends.

   ___ I ask God to help me do this step.

2. Paul, in his letter to the Ephesians, wrote about reconciliation. He described how Jesus has made two separated parties into one. Jesus has done the uniting, he says, and broken down the barrier between them:

   > But now, in Christ Jesus, you who once were far away have been brought near through the blood of Christ. For He Himself is our peace, who has made the two one and has destroyed the barrier, the dividing wall of hostility ... His purpose was to create in Himself one new man out of the two, thus making peace, and in this one body to reconcile both of them to God through the cross, by which He put to death their hostility ... Consequently, you are no longer foreigners and aliens, but fellow citizens with God's people and members of God's household, built on the foundation of the apostles

and prophets, with Christ Jesus Himself as the chief cornerstone.

—based on Ephesians 2:13–22

____ God has taken the initiative in calling me back into a relationship with Himself.
____ I am no longer a foreigner or alien. I am a citizen of heaven.
____ Jesus has broken down the wall between me and my "brother."
____ He has taken away the hostility and replaced it with His peace.
____ I am willing to go share that peace with my "brother".

3. Paul writes about our right, privilege, and call to be reconcilers. Paul and Jesus make reconciliation one of the highest priorities:

> Therefore, if anyone is in Christ, he is a new creation; the old has gone, the new has come! All this is from God, who reconciled us to Himself through Christ and gave us the ministry of reconciliation that God was reconciling the world to Himself in Christ, not counting men's sins against them. And He has committed to us the message of reconciliation. We are therefore Christ's ambassadors, as though God were making His appeal through us. We implore you on Christ's behalf: Be reconciled to God.
>
> —based on 2 Corinthians 5:17–20

____ God has made me a new creation by calling me into a relationship with Himself.
____ He has now given me the privilege of being a friend-maker and an ambassador for Him.
____ He is appealing to others through me, urging them to be reconciled to God.
____ I am willing to be His representative in all of my relationships.

Doing Step Nine: Do it now

Recently a high school student was called out of class by the principal. Someone from the family was waiting in the office. As the student entered, he knew something serious had happened. He was right. His father had just been killed in a car accident. The son was overwhelmed. He loved his father dearly. Both father and son were very well-known and liked in the school.

In no time, the news spread through the school. An unusual thing happened in every break between classes for the rest of that day. At each break, many kids were calling their dads to let them know they loved them.

Step Nine reminds us of the urgency in going to people to express our love and concern. Don't hesitate. The importance of being reunited with others cannot be overemphasized. The need is indescribable. Nothing can surpass the wonderful feelings of having restored relationships, of being reconciled.

One of our main purposes in life is to have healthy relationships with those God has gifted us with. If we are doing the ninth step with someone, it means we are taking the initiative to improve, strengthen, or restore the relationship. It means we are taking the leadership. We are creating the agenda. We are making an investment in that person. All of this is very positive.

We initially make contact with that person to ask for their permission to meet. We let them know we are not expecting anything from them. We let them know we care about the relationship and that our motivation to meet is to talk about what we could do to enhance the relationship.

We go to express our feelings, our apologies, our sorrow about the broken relationship. Sometimes we need to go to ask forgiveness. If they have harmed us in any way, we need to ask for God's help to forgive them before we meet with them.

We go without expecting anything in return from the other person. Their response is their response--we cannot control it. It would be best if they accept your apology. But they may not. You cannot do anything about that. They may reject you. That is the risk you will take. However, you will be at peace inside because you did what you could to improve the relationship.

Step Nine gives us an excuse to go to others. Usually, our strongest and best relationships are the ones that have had a reconciliation, ones where the two parties have come back together after a time of disagreement. Use this ninth step to get closer to the people from whom you have been separated.

Making Step Nine My Own

This section provides you with a format for integrating your feelings, responses to questions, and what you learned from this step, the Scriptures, and in your group meetings.

Date, day, and time of your writings: _____

1. At this point in my life, the major area that I am working on (For instance, actually going to make amends; I have thought about doing this for a long time; now is the time.):

_____

_____

2. Major insights I was given into my life through this step (There is great joy in restoring a relationship. I want this joy.):

_____

_____

_____

_____

3. The strongest feeling I have had as I have worked this step (A great desire to want to go do this step; a feeling of excitement and adventure):

_____

4. The action I feel called to take as a result of working this step (Go do it.):

_____

Chapter 10

DAILY

REVIEW

Step Ten:

Each day I do a review of

---

myself and my activities.

When I am wrong, I quickly

---

admit it. When I am right,

I thank God for the guidance.

I went to parochial schools for elementary and high school. I'll never forget the hard oak desks and beautifully polished oak floors. Specifically, I remember the blackboards in our classrooms.

In grade school, the blackboards were used frequently. By the end of the day, the boards were chalky white. Each day one of the students was assigned to stay after school to clean the boards with wet rags. As the rest of us left school for the day, we couldn't help but notice how cluttered and whitened the blackboards had become. Sometimes students were selected to clean the boards because of their not so pleasant behavior that day.

When we returned to school in the morning, the boards were clean. I felt I could start a new day with a clean slate. As an adult, I need simple reminders like this.

It is important for us to clean our personal boards every day. Our hearts, minds and souls need a daily cleansing, just as our bodies do. Step Ten is a reminder of the need for a daily audit. It's a reminder to live one day at time.

If I want to live peacefully with freedom from guilt, I need to spend a few minutes at the end of each day assessing what the day has been like for me. This will prevent a relational, spiritual and emotional "hangover." When we try to sleep knowing we have unfinished stuff, we are planting seeds inside our hearts, minds, and souls that will eventually grow and bear fruit. By not settling issues to the best of our ability before we go to sleep at the end of the day, we are giving power to that to person, problem, or concern. In our attempt to rest, our subconscious mind is at work grinding away at the unresolved matter. Byproducts are preoccupation when we wake up, a restless night, and an inability to focus on the freedom of enjoying a new day without the haunting cloud of what we need to do to fix the issue. All of this robs us of some of our creative energy.

Practicing the simple, brief exercise of Step Ten puts closure to the day and can spare us of all of those side effects.

Taking a daily review or doing a daily inventory is very simple: I spend the last few minutes of each day reflecting on what the day was like. I follow the pattern laid out below.

1. Recall in sequence the people you have been with or spoken with throughout the day.
2. Ask God to forgive you if you have been at fault in any of these events.
3. Forgive others if they were at fault in these events.
4. If you need to make amends in any of these situations, do so.
5. Thank God for the good things that have happened today and the guidance He has given.
6. Close the door to the day as best you can. Forgive and forget. Give thanks for another day of life.

A number of scriptural passages reinforce the need to do this daily review. The psalmist says, "Search me, O God, and know my heart ... lead me" (Psalm 139:23–24). He also says, "Lord, remember how short my time is" (Psalm 89:47). A day is a lifetime. Our lifetime is brief. Today is all we have. One day at a time, we carefully live out the moments given to us.

> A businessman was permitted to have one wish come true. After some thought he wished for a newspaper dated two years into the future. Miraculously the paper appeared in his hands. Turning to the stock reports, he made careful notes on the stocks that had shown unusual growth. He would certainly make a fortune.
>
> Then out of curiosity he looked through the paper and, scanning the obituary column, found his name in it. He had suffered a heart attack, and his funeral arrangements were spelled out in detail there before him.

> In His wisdom God hides the future from us. He
> wants us to live one day at a time. He wishes us to
> make today count.
>
> —Author Unknown

Paul says, "Judge yourselves soberly ... use your gifts ... have a profound respect for each other ... and be reconciled" (based on Romans 12:3–13). In Galatians he says, "Let each one examine his own work" (6:4). And in 1 John 1:8–2:2, we are given the reminder that if we acknowledge our sin and confess it, Jesus Christ will forgive us.

Doing a daily review or inventory is a matter of habit and discipline. It is a way of life. It is a great way to use the natural rhythm and cycle of daily life to remind us of the need to stay close to God, ourselves, and others. Step Ten helps prevent the stockpiling of anxiety, sin, and broken relationships. If we did Step Ten alone, without any of the other steps, it would bring renewal, vitality, and stability to our lives.

Let's look at what the Bible says about taking a review of ourselves, admitting when we are wrong, and thanking God when we are right.

What the Bible says about Step Ten

1. Do not think of yourself more highly than you ought

Paul wrote his letter to the Romans urging them to do an honest assessment of both their gifts and weaknesses. Paul wanted people to know and use their gifts. His writings on this subject had a sense of urgency about them. The following passage emphasizes the need for a daily review.

> *For by the grace given me I say to every one of you: Do not think of yourself more highly than you ought, but rather think of yourself with sober judgment, in accordance with*

the measure of faith God has given you. Just as each of us has one body with many members, and these members do not all have the same function, so in Christ we who are many form one body, and each member belongs to all the others. We have different gifts, according to the grace given us.

—based on Romans 12:3–6

___ It is important for me to assess myself and my behavior realistically.

___ I need to know more about my place in the "body."

___ I want to do a daily review to assess whether I am making the best use of my time and gifts.

___ I want to grow in my respect for others in the body who have different gifts.

2. Test your own actions

Paul wrote a letter to his Galatian friends to underscore the need for each person to review his or her own behavior, not anyone else's. "Each one should test his own actions. Then he can take pride in himself, without comparing himself to somebody else" (based on Galatians 6:4).

___ I am responsible for my own behavior and the assessment of that behavior.

___ I need not be concerned with what others do or what they think of me.

___ I sometimes compare myself to others.

3. Be honest and practical

To help the early Christians live fulfilling lives together, Paul gave the following practical advice to the Ephesians. These are great words for doing the tenth step.

Now your attitudes and thoughts must all be constantly changing for the better with each passing day. Every day, put on the new self, the new nature that God has given to you. Stop lying to each other; tell the truth, for we are all parts of each other and when we lie to each other we are hurting ourselves. Don't let the sun set on your anger. Deal with it. Get it resolved. Be reconciled before the end of the day or you will be giving the devil a mighty foothold. If anyone is stealing, that person must stop and begin using his or her gifts for honest work so he or she can give to others in need. Don't use bad language. Say only what is good and helpful to those you are talking to and what will give them a blessing. Don't cause the Holy Spirit sorrow by the way you live. He is the one who seals your salvation until the day of your arrival in heaven. Stop being mean, bad-tempered, and angry. Quarreling, harsh words, and dislike of others should have no place in your lives. Instead, be kind to each other, tenderhearted, forgiving one another, just as God has forgiven you because you belong to Christ Jesus.

—based on Ephesians 4:23–32

____ I need God's help to make the changes this passage suggests.

____ I want to use this passage for my daily review.

____ I'm not ready to do any of this stuff yet.

Now that I have read these passages, the idea of doing a daily review of myself and my activities seems:

____ tedious. I really don't have the time for it.

____ terrific. I've done it for years. It's the only way to live.

____ exciting, but I don't know how to do it.

___ to be a great idea, but I know myself well enough to know
    I'll never do it.
___ like something I want to develop.

When I am wrong, I generally
___ deny it.
___ avoid it.
___ pretend it didn't happen.
___ admit it.
___ find someone else to blame.
___ ask forgiveness.

More suggestions for how to do Step Ten

Each day I do a review of myself and my activities. When I am wrong, I quickly admit it. When I am right, I thank God for the guidance.

1: Do a daily inventory

In just a few minutes at the end of each day, you can do the daily inventory below. Use the form to help you get started. When we do a daily review, four simple and basic principles given to us by Jesus are the ultimate test of whether we are living a rich and full life. These are some of the greatest passages from the Bible. All daily reviews could include these principles.

Jesus said you must:

1. "Love the Lord your God with all your heart, with all your soul, and with all your mind" (Matthew 22:37)
2. "Love your neighbor as yourself" (Matthew 22:39)
3. "Love your enemies"
4. "Pray for those who ... persecute you" (Matthew 5:44)

117

One way to do a daily review is to look at these four passages and simply ask yourself, "Have I lived by each of these principles today?"

2: **Another way to do a daily review is to look at what Paul has written in two of his letters. Both of these are great daily review resources.**

Paul wrote a "love letter" to the Corinthians. You've probably heard it read at weddings. Now you can use it for a daily review of your life.

___ Today, have I been patient?

___ Today, have I been kind?

___ Today, have I been jealous?

___ Today, have I been boastful or conceited?

___ Today, have I been rude or selfish?

___ Today, have I taken offense or been resentful?

___ Today, have I taken pleasure in other people's sins or misfortunes?

___ Today, have I delighted in the truth?

___ Today, did I trust God and others?

___ Today, did I express hope?

___ Today, did I endure what came my way?

___ Today, did I love without conditions?

—based on 1 Corinthians 13:4–8

3: **In his letter to the Galatians, Paul listed what he called the "fruit of the Spirit" (5:22–23). These "fruits" were the evidence that a person was a Christian. Use these daily to evaluate your life.**

The fruits of the Holy Spirit:

___ Today, have I been loving?

___ Today, have I been filled with joy?

____ Today, have I been at peace?
____ Today, have I been patient?
____ Today, have I been kind?
____ Today, have I demonstrated goodness?
____ Today, have I been trustful?
____ Today, have I been gentle?
____ Today, have I demonstrated self-control?

No one is capable of having or doing all of these in his or her own power. We all need Jesus Christ to come into our lives and give us hearts that will be able to do all these important things. When we receive Jesus Christ, He gives us the ability to do what He asks of us. He wouldn't ask us to do something we're not capable of doing with Him living inside of us. He, living in us, gives us the ability to love, to pray, and to give of ourselves.

As our relationship with Jesus grows, our ability to love also grows. The more we get to know His love for us, the more we can love other people around us, even if they don't love us in return.

Making Step Ten My Own

This section provides you with a format for integrating your feelings, responses to questions, and what you learned from this step, the Scriptures, and in your group meetings.

Date, day, and time of your writings: _____

1. At this point in my life, the major area that I am working on (For instance, the challenge of doing a daily review. I know I need it. I know it will take some effort on my part to do it.):

_____

_____

2. Major insights I was given into my life through this step (The importance of checking in with myself and God each day):

_____

_____

_____

_____

3. The strongest feeling I have had as I have worked this step (Hope—I feel hopeful about what this daily review will do for me):

_____

4. The action I feel called to take as a result of working this step (To do a daily review):

_____

Chapter 11

My Most

Important

Daily

Appointment

Step Eleven:

To keep growing in my relationship

---

with Jesus Christ, I spend time

---

each day praying and reading the

Bible. I will gather with others who

---

do the same. I ask Jesus for

---

guidance and the power to do

---

what He wants me to do.

Sitting in my office for about the tenth time was a very handsome twenty-nine-year-old man. All the young women in the area noticed and talked about him. He was one of the most unusual young persons I had known. When he talked, his words had integrity. He had been raised in a healthy, loving family. Though his father was a driven financier, Joe seemed to survive with the minimal amount of time his dad gave him.

As we explored the areas of his life that he felt needed attention, we seldom found any problem or issue he had not openly identified and was not already dealing with.

"I want more than anything else to live my life for Jesus Christ. He has loved me so much, the least I can do in response is give Him my life," he said.

Often when people use that kind of "heavy Christian language," people mistrust their sincerity. When this guy talked like that, his words were authentic. He was the real deal.

"I could spend the rest of my life looking at myself. I don't want that. I want to look at Jesus. I want to look at others. I want my life to count for something. I think the way it will count for something is if I use my gifts in serving others." He said all this emphatically. He was sincere.

"I don't want to get stuck on myself. I truly want to be a disciple of Christ. What does it mean to be a disciple at this point in history?" he asked.

This young man was a very mature person for his age. He had already outgrown the need to be "successful" or accumulate material things. His life was focused on all the right things.

He had gone through the step process many times in various forms. He had worked the steps and grown immensely. He could relate very well to others in his personal and professional life.

Because he had done so much work with the steps, he did not live his life in compartments. He was the same person on Monday as he was on Sunday. He was a congruent person: His words, his feelings, and his attitude matched his behavior.

"It's what the eleventh step teaches that is making me feel so healthy," he said. "This step is the single most important step I can do for myself. I spend the first time of the day in prayer and reading the Bible. Usually that's about an hour. It has become the most important hour in my day.

"I know I'm young," he said, "but I think I'm ready to keep moving toward the things that God wants me to do.

"And I study the Bible," he continued. "I carry a verse from the Bible with me every day. I read it often. I pray about it. When it's appropriate, I share that verse with one of my friends at work or socially.

"Each week, I get together with a small group of guys from my church. We talk about what's going on in our lives. We use these steps to help us focus. And we pray for each other," he said. "I've been doing this ever since I was in high school. I couldn't live without my brothers and sisters. I need their support."

This young man stands on a solid foundation. He is ready to do whatever God wants him to do. He is beyond "recovery" and into the great things that life has to offer.

He takes Step Eleven each day. He practices the four parts of this step:

- Keep a daily appointment with God.
- Read the Bible.
- Gather with others who pray and read the Bible.
- Ask Jesus for power to do what He wants us to do.

Understanding the clear and simple characteristics of Step Eleven is easy. *Doing* them is quite another thing. Step Eleven reminds us that if we want a close relationship with Jesus Christ, we will need to spend time with Him each day. Time in prayer and reading the Bible is essential to intimacy with God.

Gathering with others to share our lives, experiences, and insights is also essential to maintaining a good relationship with

Jesus Christ. The world is trying to convince us that spiritual and eternal things don't really count. We need to be with other Christians who remind us that God is alive and real.

"What my friends do for me is alert me to the power that the world has," he went on to say. "Without my Christian friends, I could easily be convinced that I'll find the good life in having new cars, clothes, and houses. I thank God that I'm growing out of that phase."

Part of our daily prayer and reading is to seek the guidance that Jesus gives to us moment by moment and day by day. Prayer prepares us to receive His guidance. It alerts us to His presence. It shapes our character.

Another part of our daily prayer and reading is to be open to the power that Jesus will give us. Jesus instructed His disciples to wait in Jerusalem until they received the Holy Spirit and power. In much the same way, I believe, Jesus wants us to wait until He fills us with His Holy Spirit––day by day.

The Bible has much to say about the importance of prayer.

What the Bible says about Step Eleven

> Ask and you will receive; seek, and you will find; knock, and the door will be opened to you. The one who asks will receive, and anyone who seeks will find, and the door will be opened to the person who knocks.
>
> There is no need to worry. If there is anything you need, pray for it, asking God for it with prayer and thanksgiving, and that peace of God which is so much greater than we can understand will guard your hearts and minds in Christ Jesus.
>
> Pray constantly.
>
> Very early, long before daylight, Jesus got up and left the house. He went out to a lonely place, where He prayed.

The Spirit comes to help us pray, weak as we are.
For we don't know how to pray. The Spirit pleads
with God for us in groans that words cannot express.
... for where two or three meet in My name, I will
be there with them.

—based on Matthew 7:7–9;
Philippians 4:6–7;
1 Thessalonians 5:17;
Luke 4:42;
Romans 8:26;
Matthew 18:20

Think about how you spend your time every day.
How would you like to spend your time?
Are you wasting time?

As Paul was instructing the Romans to pray, he wrote:

The Spirit helps us in our weakness. We do not know
what we ought to pray for, but the Spirit Himself
intercedes for us with groans that words cannot
express. And He who searches our hearts knows the
mind of the Spirit, because the Spirit intercedes for
the saints in accordance with God's will. And we
know that in all things God works for the good of
those who love Him, who have been called according
to His purpose.

—based on Romans 8:26–27

____ I am comforted to know I do not need to be an expert in
prayer.
____ I believe the Holy Spirit will come to intercede on my behalf.
____ This is an encouraging passage for me.

In some of his teaching to young Timothy, Paul spells out the need and type of prayer that is to be offered:

> I urge, then, first of all, that requests, prayers, intercession, and thanksgiving be made for everyone--for kings and all those in authority, that we may live peaceful and quiet lives in all godliness and holiness. This is good and pleases God our Savior, who wants all men to be saved and to come to a knowledge of the truth. For there is one God and one mediator between God and men, the man Christ Jesus, who gave Himself as a ransom for all people-- the testimony given in its proper time.
>
> —based on 1 Timothy 2: 1–6

____ Lord God, help me to pray for others.

____ The amount of time I devote to prayer for others is the one area of my life I feel good about.

____ Prayer for others--this is what Jesus, the one mediator between God and people, wants from me.

The author of the Epistle to the Hebrews reminded the Hebrew Christians of their need to gather and encourage each other. This author was especially sensitive about the urgency to do so in light of the final day when Jesus would return: "And let us consider how we may encourage one another on toward love and good deeds. Let us not give up meeting together, as some are in the habit of doing, but let us encourage one another--and all the more as you see the Day approaching" (based on Hebrews 10:24–25).

____ I need the encouragement that comes from meeting with others who pray, follow Jesus, and read the Bible.

____ I have all the encouragement I need.

____ Jesus, I need to meet with my brothers and sisters. Help me to develop and keep this habit.

After reading these passages, how do you feel about praying?

____ I don't know how to do it.
____ I haven't really tried it.
____ I want to learn more about it.
____ I am undecided about prayer.

The healthiest people I know read the Bible every day.

Try reading it first thing in the morning and last thing at night. Read the passages in this book. Use a modern translation of the Bible (like The Life Application Bible or The New International Bible).

You can also purchase Bible apps from OliveTree.com.

There are many other helpful resources available online. You can go to ScriptureUnion.org or WordLive.org and request that they email a reading to you every day.

Step Eleven is crucial because it addresses our lifestyle and challenges us to put first things first. When our priorities are right, our lives will be coherent, "together." Fragmentation makes us frustrated and anxious because it pulls us in many directions at the same time. Daily prayer helps us focus on what's most important to God.

Occasionally, we also need prayer retreats, half days or days devoted to solitude, giving us added time to reflect on God's love.

Making Step Eleven My Own

This section provides you with a format for integrating your feelings, responses to questions, and what you learned from this step, the Scriptures, and in your group meetings.

Date, day, and time of your writings: _____

1. At this point in my life, the major area that I am working on (For instance, I need to meet with others who want to pray and read the Bible.):

_____

_____

2. Major insights I was given into my life through this step (I need to be more deliberate in my personal discipline so that I can grow spiritually.):

_____

_____

_____

_____

3. The strongest feeling I have had as I have worked this step (Encouragement—I am more eager than ever to begin and continue a daily "program" for prayer.):

_____

4. The action I feel called to take as a result of working this step (Call two friends to talk with them about getting together on a weekly basis to pray.):

_____

Chapter 12

I WILL REACH

OUT TO

OTHERS

Step Twelve:

I am grateful God is

---

changing me through these

Twelve Steps. In response,

I will reach out to share Christ's

---

love by practicing these

---

principles in all I do.

In our training workshops, I often tell the story of a man who lived in San Francisco and had decided to end his life. All his circumstances led to despondency. For him, it was simply a matter of how he would end it.

Several days went by as he thought about the ways to commit suicide. The first option he considered was to go to his office bathroom, cut his wrists, and die there. Concerned that this might be messy, he thought about another option. He would jump out of his thirteenth floor office window. This would be a quick way to end it all. On second thought, kind as he was, he remembered the possibility of landing on someone and taking that person's life as well.

As he pondered this some more, another idea came to him. It would be best to jump off the bridge. Ah, that was it. That was simplest and cleanest. He put on his coat and mentally said good-bye to his office and belongings and quietly headed out to the elevator.

As the elevator moved down to the first floor, he heard a voice say, "Give life just one more chance." Conscientious as he was, he obeyed and made a decision to do just that. *If the next person I see when I get off this elevator smiles at me and greets me, that will be my sure sign that life deserves another chance,* he said to himself.

Are you the next person Steve will see?

Experience tells us there are hundreds of people out there who are looking for some kind of reassuring sign that life is worth living. Our simple smile and greeting could save their lives.

Step Twelve is about reaching out and giving ourselves to others as well as clarifying your purpose and course for life.

All of the work you have done in the first eleven steps will help you to see more clearly how you are to invest your life. Each step you have taken has demonstrated your desire to cooperate with Him. When we are faithful in little things, He gives us greater things.

When we surrender a bit to Him, He gives us a great deal more back.

Step Twelve urges us to move out and give.

There are seasons in our lives when we need to pull back and do nothing but take good care of ourselves (Steps One through Eleven). There is also a time to thank God for what He has done to restore and prepare us–and then get into a season of giving to others.

So the twelfth step is done by those who:

1. receive Jesus Christ day by day and moment by moment. They take in all He has to give to them. They gratefully accept His grace and initiative in their lives;

2. make up their minds they are needed and must serve others. They become convinced they can do this service. Jesus said they will do "greater works" (John 14:12). Paul says, "I can do all things through Christ who strengthens me" (Philippians 4:13). They believe these passages and put them into action;

3. know their gifts and talents, and they are open to where God wants them to use these. They go out and find their spot (which most likely is where they are already), beginning in their own homes, and then serving other family, fellow employees, neighbors, and acquaintances;

4. serve. They do little things, which leads to doing bigger things.

Jesus Himself did this. The first thirty years of His life were spent in preparation for ministry. And then He moved out into the world.

Paul spent fourteen years in preparation and then moved out into a phenomenal ministry.

To get healthy, we all need a time of retreat and recovery and then we need to move out into the front lines sharing who we are and what we have been given.

Jesus serves His disciples

They were at their last supper together. His betrayer was at the table with Him, along with the other eleven disciples.

Jesus got up from the table, removed His outer garment, and took a towel and wrapped it around His waist. He then poured water into a basin and began to wash the disciples' feet and to wipe them with the towel He was wearing.

Peter said to Him, "Lord, are you going to wash my feet?"

Jesus answered, "At the moment you do not know what I am doing, but later you will understand."

"Never," said Peter. "You will never wash my feet."

Jesus replied, "If I do not wash you, you can have nothing in common with Me."

When He had washed their feet and put on His clothes again, He went back to the table. "Do you understand," He said, "what I have done to you? You call me Master and Lord and rightly so--I am. If I, then, the Lord and Master has washed your feet, you should wash each other's feet. I have given you an example so that you may copy what I have done to you.

"I tell you the truth, no servant is greater than his master, and no messenger is greater than the man who sent him. Now that you know this, happiness will be yours if you do this" (based on John 13:3–17).

1. The message for me from this reading is about
    ___ having faith ("You do not understand now, but you will understand.").
    ___ servanthood.
    ___ being a model teacher.
    ___ learning how to wash the feet of others.

2. The main reason I don't serve others more is
___ I don't know where the need is.
___ I don't know how to serve others.
___ I don't know how to begin. I want to serve, but I need help in getting started.
___ I don't have time for serving others. My hands are full already.
___ Serving others is not my gift.
___ Serving others is not a priority for me.

3. If I had been Peter and Jesus had come to wash my feet, I
___ would have reacted just as Peter did––originally refused to let Jesus wash my feet.
___ would have been very threatened by this act of servanthood. If Jesus did that for me, it would mean I would have to do the same for others.
___ would not have thought much about it. I would have simply let Jesus do as He had planned.
___ would have been very humbled by this experience.

So, how do you feel about the Twelve-Step Process at this point?

To the best of my knowledge, here is my own assessment of where I am with the Twelve Steps:
___ These steps have helped me a great deal.
___ I am now ready to serve others by reaching out to share the love of Christ with them.
___ I need another go-around with the steps. Right now I feel inadequate to reach out. I need more time. (Some people need years.)
___ I am working at putting these principles to work on a daily basis. They are working for me.
___ I am eager to share what I have learned with others. I am looking for a place to do that.

133

Just as Jesus served others, He also asked His disciples to serve those who needed help.

The young man who was called to serve

A man came running up to Jesus, knelt before Him, and asked Him this question: "Good Master, what must I do to inherit eternal life?"

Jesus said to him, "You know the commandments; You must not kill; you must not commit adultery; you must not steal; you must not cheat; you must not bear false witness; honor your father and mother."

And the young man said to Him, "Master, I have carefully kept these commandments from my earliest days. What is still missing in my life?"

Jesus looked steadily at him and loved him, and He said, "There is one thing you lack. Go and sell everything you own and give the money to the poor, and you will have treasures in heaven. Then come follow Me." But the young man's face fell at these words and he went away sad, for he was a man of great wealth (based on Mark 10:17–22).

1. Why do you think the rich young man came to Jesus?
   ____ He was looking for another way to make money.
   ____ He was empty. He knew something was missing in his life.
   ____ He wanted to find a sure way to heaven.

2. Which of Jesus's responses to the rich young man impressed you the most?
   ____ That Jesus loved him.
   ____ That Jesus told him how to solve his problem: go sell what he had and give the money to the poor.
   ____ That Jesus called him to come and follow Him.

3. Even though the rich young man had carefully kept the commandments from early in his life, one thing was still missing for him. What do you think it was?

___ His heart was not surrendered to God.

___ He was good and he was religious, but he had not "sold out" to God.

___ His wealth was an obstacle.

___ He did not have a relationship with Jesus Christ.

4. At this point in the Twelve Steps, what is the one thing still missing in your life?

___ My wealth is an obstacle for me.

___ I am not willing to sell everything I have and give the money to the poor.

___ Eternal life is not that big of a deal to me.

___ I don't have a good relationship with Jesus Christ.

___ I don't care much about poor people.

___ I am afraid to be "sold out" to God.

What the Bible says about Step Twelve

After His resurrection, Jesus showed up on the shoreline of Tiberias. He provided some bread and a fish dinner for the disciples after they had caught nothing on a fishing trip.

> When they had finished eating, Jesus said to Simon Peter,
> "Simon, son of John, do you truly love Me more than these?"
> "Yes, Lord," he said, "you know that I love You."
> Jesus said, "Feed My lambs."
> Again Jesus said, "Simon, son of John, do you truly love Me?"
> He answered, "Yes, Lord, you know that I love You."
> Jesus said, "Take care of My sheep."
> The third time He said to him, "Simon son of John, do you love Me?"

Peter was hurt because Jesus asked him the third time,
"Do you love Me?" He said, "Lord, You know all things; You
know that I love You."
Jesus said, "Feed My sheep."

—based on John 21: 15–17

____ I am overwhelmed with this assignment of feeding sheep
but know Jesus will give me the strength I need.

____ I believe Jesus knows all things

____ I love Jesus Christ.

____ I want to feed the sheep He has called me to serve in my
home, work, and church.

Beyond ourselves

I was fifteen years old when I first *heard* of the Twelve Steps. At
that age, hearing about "steps" to anything meant nothing. I was a
typical teenager: I had an independent spirit. I was trying out my
wings. I was tired of being told how to live life.

Through Alateen and Al-Anon, I *saw* the Twelfth Step in motion.
I saw people who lived out the Twelve-Step lifestyle. They talked
about it and they lived it. When someone in their group had a need,
they helped each other. They were there to support each other
emotionally. They helped meet each other's financial needs. They
stood by each other prayerfully.

I was involved with some Al-Anon people who invested much
of their time, energy, and money in developing a great treatment
center for chemically dependent people and their families. They
served unselfishly. They were always available to share parts of
their stories that might be helpful to individuals or families.

I saw people in pain reaching out to each other. Suffering
families found hope in being with others who had similar problems.
Individuals were sharing themselves and their stories with each
other. Recovering alcoholics were going out to meet with active

alcoholics to tell them their stories and to share the good news: that recovery is possible and there is another way of life.

A therapist friend of mind often says, "I wish all families could have the privilege of getting the kind of help alcoholic's families can get."

Seeing these folks' support for each other gave me a vision and model that has been deeply integrated into who I am. I have a clear idea of what genuine community can look like.

My spiritual formation began in parochial schools. After opening my life to Jesus Christ, receiving Him, and developing a relationship with Him, I continued to grow in healthy, prayerful Catholic spirituality alongside solid, evangelical, scriptural growth. Subtly and gently, the Twelve-Step process has been there as a part of this growth. The Twelve-Step process is a natural part of Christian formation.

In my experience, all the previous eleven steps build toward this twelfth step. I am most alive and excited about life when I am sharing with others. When I am giving of myself to others, I feel best about myself. When I am exercising my gifts for the benefit of others, I am energized.

The twelfth step is an action step. It challenges me to give as others have given to me. All of us have made it this far because others have given to us. Now it is our turn to give in response.

This giving is not only material things; it is simple and small things. It involves holding a door, saying an encouraging word, complimenting someone, writing a note, calling a friend, shoveling a neighbor's walk, or volunteering at a local food shelf.

Step Twelve challenges us to leave the comfortable. It nudges us to move out into the hurting world to bring healing, light, and Jesus Christ. He is the bread of life that all the world seeks. We are His hands and feet.

We must go beyond ourselves and our group. We must go––to love, to give, and to serve. The problems we all have experienced earlier in our lives provided opportunities to grow and to experience

God's love and healing so that we would be equipped to share that love with others.

Step Twelve is an action step. It's about doing, moving out, and going. We are to reach out and share with others that which has been given to us in love.

In some ways the first eleven steps are essentially preparation for Step Twelve--the first eleven free us up so we can serve Christ and others.

To be a follower of Christ means we have chosen to deny ourselves, to take up our cross, to follow Him. Being a follower of Christ means more than being "spiritual." Being a follower of His means we are "into" Christ, the Person, and He is "in" us, and we follow where He leads--into the world that needs us to share Him.

We have chosen a path of surrender and service. It is our way of life. We seek to love as we have been loved. We seek to serve as Jesus served us. We seek to put our faith into action.

Doing Step Twelve

I am grateful that God is changing me through these Twelve Steps. In response, I will reach out to share Christ's love by practicing these principles in all that I do.

Check below those areas that you personally will do something about:

____   Write a note to my parents.

____   Write a note to my spouse.

____   Offer to share my resources.

____   Volunteer my time to help where I am needed.

____   Write letters to lonely relatives.

____   Tell my friends about Jesus Christ.

____   Buy and take a Bible to them.

____   Write notes to my children.

____   Call someone to let them know I am thinking of them.

___ Start a group using these steps.
___ Invite a friend to that group.
___ Write a note to a coworker.
___ Help a friend with a project.
___ Write a letter to a missionary.
___ Give someone some of my clothes.
___ Give something valuable away.
___ Give more to my church
___ Today, pray for everyone in my neighborhood.
___ Pray for one country in the world every day.
___ Make arrangements to visit someone in prison.
___ Give my friend a Bible for his/her birthday.
___ Work on a project to help others.
___ Go visit shut-ins.
___ "Adopt" a grandparent.
___ Befriend a lonely or rejected child or teenager.
___ Visit a hospital.
___ Serve as a hospice volunteer.
___ Pray for my ministers and staff. Offer to serve them.

And there are greater ways in which we can give to fulfill the challenge of the twelfth step:

- Fulfilling our life mission
- Doing our best in our profession
- Serving others the best we can
- Taking risks in exploring ways to make better use of our lives, gifts, and talents.

These we work at one day at a time, one moment at a time.

As Christians, we have a clear call: to bring the message of Jesus Christ to others all around the world. Many missionaries have a call to serve others in a foreign land. We each have our own mission work. It may be someone in our church, our next door neighbor, or a distant relative. We have the wonderful privilege of handing on the good news to others: Christ is here. Christ is alive. Jesus loves us and accepts us just as we are. What more could anyone want?

My participation in small group meetings has given me more than I can comprehend. It has given me unconditional acceptance, affirmation, support, encouragement, new vision, and renewed hope. As I meet with a group that uses this framework, I am given the nourishment I need to go back out to my family, profession, and friendships. I am renewed and strengthened to love those I am with--even those who may sometimes be unlovable.

The final benefit of the Steps to New Life Process

The older I get, the more I am aware of the need for healthy, clear voices to speak into the darkness of our times.

Our culture needs women and men whose lives are well integrated, balanced, healthy, and congruent. These times demand more integrity from men and women than ever before in the history of America.

The world needs true disciples of Jesus Christ as it never has before.

True disciples don't become "true" by simply going to church, affirming a specific doctrine, or going to Bible studies. True disciples need more than that. They need a way to become whole, healthy, and integrated. They need a lifestyle based on and patterned after Jesus Christ.

We must all learn again what it means to be a whole person. We must all return again to those years when our grandparents held us in their arms, sat in rocking chairs, and told us simple stories. We need again that kind of parenting, encouragement, direction, and guidance. We need once again to discover sincere compassion--basic concern and caring for our families, neighbors, and others.

This book will draw us back into the basics. It will point us in the direction of the simple life. It will get us into a process that will make us more aware of our vulnerabilities and our need to express them to others. It will help us discern what life is really like for us.

We all need something like the Twelve-Step process. Without such a framework, we will too easily become our own gods, designing our lives and our own agendas as we think they should be. These other gods will eventually bring us down. We have no business trying to run our own or anyone else's life.

As we quoted earlier in this book, the well-known poster cites two fundamental realities in life:

1. There is a God;
2. You are not Him.

This book and this process have hopefully been a simple reminder of those fundamental realities.

Jesus said we should enter by the narrow gate, since the road that leads to hell is wide and spacious and many take it; but it is a narrow gate and a hard road that leads to life and only a few find it (see Matthew 7:13–14).

This Twelve-Step process helps readers find the narrow gate. It encourages participants to stay on the hard road. We are fellow travelers on this journey into life. We need each other and this process. It will hold us accountable for our past, present, and future life.

As you go forward into this process and become even more molded and shaped by the love and grace of Jesus Christ, it is my prayer that you will experience great relief, joy, and freedom as thousands of others and I have done.

Making Step Twelve My Own

This section provides you with a format for integrating your feelings, responses to questions, and what you learned from this step, the Scriptures, and in your group meetings.

Date, day, and time of your writings: _____

1. At this point in my life, the major area that I am working on (For instance, finding a specific person I can reach out to day by day.):

_____

_____

2. Major insights I was given into my life through this step (I need to serve more.):

_____

_____

_____

_____

3. The strongest feeling I have had as I have worked this step (An urgency to get out and serve):

_____

4. The action I feel called to take as a result of working this step (Specifically, make a call today to an elderly, distant relative. I will offer to help her with the maintenance in her home.):

_____

Steps to discovering your course for life with Scriptural references

Step 1:   I admit I am powerless over certain parts of my life and I need God's help.

> **Romans 5:6--We were powerless, when at just the right time, Christ died for us.**

Step 2:   I am coming to believe that Jesus Christ came in a human body, that He is here with me now in Spirit, and that He has the power to change my weaknesses into strengths.

> **Colossians 1:15–17--Jesus Christ is the visible expression of the invisible God. All things were created by Him and for Him, and He holds all things in unity.**

Step 3:   I turn my will and my life over to Jesus Christ, my Lord and Savior.

> **Galatians 2:20--I have been crucified with Christ. It is no longer I who live, but Christ who lives in me. And the life, which I now live in the flesh, I live by faith in the Son of God who loved me and gave Himself for me.**

Step 4: I begin honestly listing what I know and discover about myself: my strengths, weaknesses, needs and behavior.

> **Psalm 139:14, 23--I am wonderful and my soul knows this very well. Lord, examine me and know my heart. Probe me and know my thoughts. Make sure I do not follow harmful ways.**

Step 5: I am ready to honestly share with God and another person the exact nature of my strengths, weaknesses, and behavior.

> **James 5:16--Confess your sins to one another and pray for one another. In this way you will be healed.**

Step 6: I am entirely ready to have Jesus Christ heal all those areas of my life that need His touch.

> **Mark 6:56b--All those who touched Jesus were healed.**

Step 7: I humbly ask Jesus Christ to change my weaknesses into strengths so I will become more like Him.

> **1 John 1:9--If we acknowledge our sin, He is faithful and just. He will forgive us and purify us from everything that is wrong.**

Step 8: I make a list of the people I have hurt and become willing to go to them to mend the relationship.

> **John 13:34–35—By the love that you have for one another, the world will know that you are My disciples.**

Step 9:   I make amends with the people I have hurt, except when to do so might bring harm to them or others.

> **Matthew 5:23–24—If you remember that your brother/sister has something against you, leave your offering there before the altar, go and be reconciled to your brother/sister first and then come back and present your offering.**

Step 10:   Each day I do a review of myself and my activities. When I am wrong, I quickly admit it. When I am right, I thank God for the guidance.

> **Galatians 6:4—Let each examine his own conduct.**

Step 11:   To keep growing in my relationship with Jesus Christ, I spend time each day praying and reading the Bible. I will gather with others who do the same. I ask Jesus for guidance and the power to do what He wants me to do.

> **John 15:7—Remain in Me. If you remain in Me and My words abide in you, you may ask what you will and you will get it.**

Step 12:   I am grateful that God is changing me through these Twelve Steps. In response, I will reach out to share

Christ's love by practicing these principles in all that I do.

Matthew 25:40--Whatever you did to the least of My brothers/sisters, you did it to Me.

Profile for Ron Keller, Ph.D.

Ron Keller has been a full time counselor/corporate consultant for more than 40 years. He is passionate about helping individuals, corporate and non-profit leaders discover their uniqueness and then capitalize on that uniqueness to accomplish more than they could ever imagine or hope for. He has counseled, consulted and worked with leaders, teams and employees from all professions.

Ron has a Bachelors in Business, an MA in Theology and a Ph.D. in Counseling Psychology. He is the author of several books, two of them previously published by Thomas Nelson Publishing in Nashville.

Ron and his wife, Nancy, live in Minneapolis, Minnesota. In addition to their private practice and professional roles, they have invested in marriages and engaged couples through counseling, hundreds of workshops and sailing retreats for 25 years.

GO TO RONKELLERASSOCIATES.COM

THE DISCOVER YOUR COURSE FOR LIFE COURSE
RETREATS
WORKSHOPS
SPEAKING ENGAGEMENTS
LEADERSHIP TRAINING